HISTORY AND COMMUNICATIONS

Harold Innis, Marshall McLuhan, the Interpretation of History

This provocative essay uses as a starting place the work of two towering figures in Canadian intellectual history: Harold Innis and Marshall McLuhan. Graeme Patterson questions conventional understanding of the thought of Innis and McLuhan and the relationship between their work.

Historians of Canada have generally considered communications an area distinct from (and irrelevant to) their own. Harold Innis is usually regarded as having moved from the field of Canadian history in his early work to non-Canadian history and communications. The distinction, Patterson suggests, is false; both the early and the late work of Innis are in the field of communications and, indeed, so is the study of history itself.

Using nineteenth-century Upper Canadian political history as a focus, Patterson applies communications theory to such familiar subjects as the Family Compact, responsible government, and the rebellion of 1837, and shows how Canadian opinion was generated and shaped by media of communication. Both Innis and McLuhan held that the technologies of writing and printing conditioned and structured human consciousness, resulting in 'literal mindedness.' Using that insight, Patterson explores the thinking of nineteenth- and twentieth-century writers of Canadian history, including Donald Creighton, J.M.S. Careless, and Chester Martin.

In his challenge to long-standing views, Patterson offers a new way of understanding the work of two key thinkers, and new ways to think about communications theory, Canadian history, historiography, and history as a discipline.

GRAEME PATTERSON is Associate Professor of History, University of Toronto.

GRAEME PATTERSON

HISTORY AND COMMUNICATIONS

Harold Innis, Marshall McLuhan, the Interpretation of History

UNIVERSITY OF TORONTO PRESS

Toronto Buffalo London

© University of Toronto Press 1990
Toronto   Buffalo   London
Printed in Canada

ISBN 0-8020-2764-4 (cloth)
ISBN 0-8020-6810-3 (paper)

Printed on acid-free paper

Canadian Cataloguing in Publication Data

Patterson, Graeme H., 1934-
History and communications

ISBN 0-8020-2764-4 (bound) ISBN 0-8020-6810-3 (pbk.)

1. Canada – Historiography.   2. Historiography.
3. Information theory in historiography.
4. Innis, Harold A., 1894-1952.
5. McLuhan, Marshall, 1911-1980.   I. Title

FC149.P37 1990   971'.0072   C90-094548-6
F1024.P37 1990

This book has been published with the help of a grant
from the Social Science Federation of Canada,
using funds provided by the Social Sciences and
Humanities Research Council of Canada.

CONTENTS

ACKNOWLEDGMENTS

I wish to thank Professor John Sipe from whom I have from time to time sought advice with respect to modern physics. Most of this book was read in manuscript form by my friend Matthew Sheard, who offered helpful advice.

I thank Corinne McLuhan for permission to quote from the H.M. McLuhan Papers, Mr Wilfred Watson for permission to quote from a letter he wrote to H.M. McLuhan, Anne Innis Dagg, Hugh Innis, Mary Innis Cates, and Wendy Innis for permission to quote from the Harold Innis Papers, Michael Easterbrook for permission to quote from the W.T. Easterbrook Papers, the Creighton estate for permission to quote from an unpublished manuscript in the D.G. Creighton Papers, and the *New Yorker* for permission to use the cartoon on page 109. The excerpt on page 176 from 'Burnt Norton' in *Four Quartets*, copyright 1943 by T.S. Eliot and renewed 1971 by Esmé Valerie Eliot, is reprinted by permission of Harcourt Brace Jovanovich, Inc., and Faber and Faber Ltd.

ONE

HAROLD INNIS AND THE INTERPRETATION OF HISTORY

I

It is generally agreed that the early work of Harold Innis has had a very considerable influence upon Canadian historical thought. Ramsay Cook, rightly arguing that a historiographical 'Innis revolution' resulted from it, has contended: 'The necessary starting-point for any clear understanding of the outlook of contemporary English-Canadian historians is Harold Adams Innis.'[1] No one, however, has argued that the 'late work' of Innis has had any such influence. Yet, while contemporary historians of Canada may certainly be understood in terms of Innis, he (most notably in the last decade of his life) cannot fully be understood without some reference to them. And the late work is more closely related to Canadian studies than is commonly supposed.

II

In his last years Innis studied ideas and material commodities both in relation to each other and in relation to the various media by which they were communicated. 'A medium of communication,' he wrote with respect to ideas, 'has an important influence on the dissemination of knowledge over space and over time and it becomes necessary to study its characteristics in order to appraise its influence in its cultural setting.'[2] Depending upon setting – whether cultural, geographic, economic, or historic – he treated all media as possessing either a 'bias of space' or a 'bias of time,' terms that were relative to each other, not absolute. Thus rivers, canals, oceans, roads, railways, and related media, which enabled central governments to extend control over territories that Innis termed 'empires,' reflected a bias of space. On the other hand, media reflecting a bias of time were institutions with qualities that enabled them to endure over long periods of time and with interests that were either localized or non-territorial. Here, for example, he had in mind the priesthoods of ancient Egypt, the satrapies of Persia, the provinces of Rome, and the Christian church. Institutions such as these were sustained by power that might be related to regional interest or to monopoly control of some commodity, such as papyrus, or of some form of knowledge, such as literacy. Sometimes in their own interests these institutions served the central governments of empire; and sometimes, for the same reason, they opposed them. And central governments, in their interest in maintaining control over space, sometimes protected and used these institutions, and sometimes tried to limit or destroy them.

Apart from all this, material media, Innis contended, had a formative influence upon their ideal content. Information mediated by clay tablets, for example, was limited in ways that did not obtain when it was mediated by newspapers. Small and heavy clay tablets were not well suited to mediating large quantities of information over space; but they were more enduring than paper. Thus clay tablets and newspapers, relative to each other, exhibited a bias of time and a bias of space. Beyond this, however, material media, according to Innis, had a formative influence upon concepts themselves – such as concepts of space and of time – that were of peculiar interest to him.

Because of his interest in studying the ideal in relation to the material, Innis's late work also reflects an interest in idealist philosophers, like Plato and Kant, and in writers of universal history, like Hegel and Marx. But he cannot be said to have belonged to any of their schools. He differed from Hegel and Marx, for example, in that he regarded 'progress' as a superstition of the mind and struggled against his own determinism. And while, like these other students of universal history, he was much concerned with the way the universe was regarded by physicists, he was interested in the modern, post-Einstein physics of relativity and rejected the mechanical, Newtonian physics of the eighteenth and nineteenth centuries. It is significant that he appears to have been completely uninterested in the epistemology of Kant, who taught that objects of experience invariably enter consciousness in the forms of space and time, intuitions prior to all forms of conceptual knowledge. He read with interest the classical sociologists, Durkheim, Weber, and their followers – whose notions of form were influenced by the *Critique of Pure Reason* – but he was concerned with *changing* concepts, and he sought his epistemology elsewhere.

' "Space and time," ' he wrote (citing F.M. Cornford), ' "and also their space-time product, fall into their places as mere mental frameworks of our own constitution." '[3] Cornford, a classicist interested in the origin of the recently outmoded Euclidean concept of space, was quoting the astronomer and mathematician Sir Arthur Eddington, who held that the true foundation of natural philosophy must be epistemology. In this sort of way, Innis was interested in the changing spatial and temporal conceptual underpinnings of historical interpretation that were also structures of the mind. Treating almost everything as media of communication, Innis included even himself – who, he himself suggested, was biased with regard to time.

For Innis, then, the world of the media was a place of complex dialectical oppositions. And in the modern world, according to him, this dialectic was hastening to a resolution of catastrophe. Technological innovation had upset a space-time balance in favour of space; flexible, holistic oral traditions had yielded to rigid, fragmenting, written and mechanical traditions; unified learning had given way to specialized knowledge; and centralized authority threatened to overcome decentralized decision making. This bias of space, he further contended, was also reflected in the present-minded, specialized concerns of contemporary scholarship.

This late work of Innis was related to his early studies of railways and waterways and staple commodities, which he viewed as having patterned the economic, social, and political experience of Canada. It also contradicted, in many respects, a set of ideas known to historians as 'the Laurentian thesis' with which the name of Innis, along with that of Donald Creighton, is usually associated. And, in many regards, it was scarcely less contradictory of the points of view, modes of thought, and assumptions of other contemporary scholars.

III

In the beginning, particularly with respect to *The Fur Trade in Canada* (1930), the work of Innis coincided with the interests of other historians. It gave an economic basis to Canadian history at a time when economic interpretations were newly fashionable both in Europe and America. In a concluding chapter of *The Fur Trade*, he treated fur in relation to other staple commodities – timber, wheat, and flour – that succeeded it in the commerce of the St Lawrence–Great Lakes communications system. He thereby distinguished between these staples and the communications system itself, a distinction of content and form that differentiated staple theory from related transportation theory.

It was the latter that related chiefly to the interests of Donald Creighton, who by the 1930s had become concerned with the commercial and political interests of certain Montreal merchants whose trade was oriented to the St Lawrence. While Creighton, like Innis, knew that the staple content of this river system was possessed of value, and that this shaped the economic, social, and political life of communities dependent upon it, this interested him less than the emergence of a centralized, mercantile 'empire' determined by that transportation system.

'The Laurentian theme,' Creighton later observed, 'has its basis in the fact that the St. Lawrence is the one great river system that leads from the Atlantic seaboard to the heart of the continent of North America,'[4] a statement that, in the language of Innis, suggests a fundamental bias of space. It was the unifying and centralizing aspects of the system that were Creighton's main concerns. Innis, on the other hand, was relatively more interested in the effects of commodities. He indicated, for example, the destructive effects of European trade goods upon Indian societies, a concern indicative of an interest in time. But Innis thought of both transportation systems and commodities as media of communication, as Creighton did not, an insight that would later be pursued by Marshall McLuhan.* In the 1930s and 1940s, however, differences of interpretation between Innis and other scholars were of no great consequence.

The problem emerged about 1950 with the publication of *Empire and Communications*. Sometimes thought to mark the beginning of the late work, this book was written one way by Innis and read in various other ways by many baffled readers. To historians of Canada the book seemed unrelated to their discipline and connected to Innis's early work chiefly by way of certain studies of the Canadian pulp and paper industry he had made in the 1940s. In the introduction to *Empire and Communications* Innis himself, however, indicated that the work was structurally related to *The Fur Trade in Canada* of 1930.

'It has seemed to me,' he wrote,

that the subject of communication offers possibilities in that it occupies a crucial position in the organization and administration of government and in turn of empires and of Western civilization. But I must confess at this point a bias which has led me to give particular attention to this subject. In studies of Canadian economic history ... I have been influenced by a phenomenon strikingly evident in Canada ... Briefly,

---

* McLuhan treated commodities as media in *Understanding Media: The Extensions of Man* (New York 1962).

North America is deeply penetrated by three vast inlets from the Atlantic – the Mississippi, the St Lawrence, and Hudson Bay, and the rivers of its drainage basin.[5]

Thus it was waterways, not pulp and paper, that directly led to the late work; although Innis intended 'to suggest that the changing character of the British Empire during the present century has been in part a result of the pulp and paper industry and its influence on public opinion ...'[6] Innis was able to perceive an analogy between a communications system of waterways and other systems having to do with the organization of governments; and this escaped most of his readers.

The early work of Innis has often been identified with that of his close friend and colleague Donald Creighton who, to be sure, was greatly influenced by him. However, Creighton's views of history, concepts of empire, and patterns of thought more generally were strikingly different from those of his friend, whose thought was much less rigidly, linearly sequential. Paper, as treated by Innis, for example, was *at once* a basic staple *and* a medium of communication. As such, it unified some of his thinking on the subject of staples and communications systems. Yet Creighton, in relating the early and late work, perceived not a unification of interest but a shift of the same.

A shift of interest, Creighton thought, had begun with the study of the Canadian pulp and paper industry. 'But immediately beyond the manufacture of pulp and paper,' he wrote, 'lay the strange and different world of journalism and the newspaper; and obviously the main stages in its modern industrial development ... had taken place not in Canada but in Great Britain and the United States'; and behind the newspaper and the book, he continued, 'were the vestiges of other, earlier forms of communication. And behind the civilization of Western Europe and America stretched a procession of older and vanished empires.'[7] This was to impose a linear concept of history upon a mind that was notoriously given to non-linear modes of thinking. The world of journalism and newspapers was not imagined to be 'strange and different' from that of pulp and paper by Innis; he thought of them as closely related and inter-dependent. Moreover, while chronological sequence was not absent from his later work, he did not visualize the civilizations he studied as merely stretching back in time in the form of a procession, for he was employing the techniques of the compar-ative historian. From Creighton's point of view, Innis's new interests seemed remote from Canadian history; and from this same vantage point it was almost impossible to see that he might be applying and testing ideas derived from Canadian history and relevant to it.

The idea that the late work was in an entirely new field of 'communications,' however, did not result from the thought of Donald Creighton. Up until the publication of *Empire and Communications* it was generally assumed that 'transportation' was 'communications.' So commonplace was that assumption that, some four years after the death of Innis, J.M.S. Careless could refer to the work of both Innis and Creighton as studies of 'essentially great systems of continent-wide communications.'[8] Certain early readers of *Empire and Communications*, however, would not allow the word to retain this meaning. ' "Communications" in Professor Innis's title,' observed the archaeologist V. Gordon Childe in the *Canadian Journal of Eco-nomics and Political Science*, 'means not "means of transport" – a rather hackneyed theme – but "communication of ideas." '[9] And the historian Arthur Maheux, writing in the *Canadian Historical Review*, reached a similar conclusion. Observing that the book's purpose was to suggest the significance of communication to modern civilization, to which end it analysed a continual conflict between the oral tradition and the written word, he added: 'Consequently the term "communication" in this book does not mean such physical avenues of communication as roads and rivers, which have been considered by other writers as the chief sources of civilization.'[10]

In view of the fact that chapter 1 of the book deals with the river culture of the Nile, and chapter 2 with civilization in relation to the Tigris and Euphrates, Maheux reached an astonishing conclusion. But the point to be noted here is that either being ignorant of, or having forgotten, the context of the early work and Innis's own assertion of its continuing relevance, neither Maheux nor Childe could understand the text before them. Waterways and roads were central to the thesis of *Empire and Communications*. Being the means whereby other media of communication – clay tablets, papyrus rolls, newspapers, and such – were transported over space, they imposed patterns upon the *spatial* dissemination of ideas.

The meaning of the word 'communications,' however, was now beginning to shift and, with this shift, there emerged a conviction that Innis had moved from the fields of economics and history into a new and essentially different field of communications. The old meaning of the term as understood by Innis and others was in the process of being lost.

This new, limited concept of communications, coupled with the notion that Innis was a joint author of the Laurentian thesis,' now began to inform historiographical thought. 'If Innis was the first to present a documented study of the Laurentian thesis,' wrote Ramsay Cook, 'Creighton first made it intelligible.'[11] 'Innis's most important work,' he also observed, 'was in the field of economic history. His later work in the nebulous field of communications may some day be judged his greatest achievement; but for historians of Canada his early studies ... will always remain the most prominent monuments in the Innis [historiographical] revolution.'[12] The 'field of communications,' however, was not nebulous; it had simply become completely befogged.

IV

In recent years some of this fog has lifted. Noting that as early as 1934 (which is to say long before the pulp and paper studies) Innis was 'outlining the relationship between public opinion, politics, and the mechanization of words in newspaper and radio,' Leslie A. Pal has concluded that 'many of Innis's substantive ideas on communications were forming in the mid-1930s.'[13] But Pal saw no relationship between ideas related to communications and others related to transportation and staples, a parallel that has been perceived by Carl Berger, who has observed that Innis, 'looked on the technology of communication in much the same way as he had looked on the staple. Technologies of communication – whether they be stone tablets, newspapers, or radios – influenced societies, institutions, and cultures in the same way that the exploitation of certain economic staples shaped them.'[14]

Berger, in contrast to Pal, did not regard *any* of the early work as being studies in communications. Because of this he thought he discerned 'an inner logic in the development of Innis's thought from the economics of the staples trades to his communications studies.' No such linear development ever took place. And the mode of thought relating the early work to that which followed it was not *logical*; it was *analogical*, as Berger's own discussion of the treatment of staples and other media suggests.

Certainly it is analogy and not logic, or any other linear form of thinking, that relates *Empire and Communications* to the studies of transportation and staples that preceded it. 'The Nile,' began Innis, 'with its irregularities of overflow, demanded a co-ordination of effort. The river created the black land which could only be exploited with a universally accepted discipline and a common goodwill of the inhabitants. The Nile acted as a principle of order and centralization, necessitated collective work, created solidarity, imposed organizations on the people, and cemented them in a society.'[15] Reading this passage, Maheux and others were unable to see that Innis was again studying a river system in relation to basic staple content. The basic staple here was silt, which structured life in ancient Egypt far more radically than fur was to structure life in New France. But Innis did not treat this basic staple merely as content. It too was a medium of communication. The medium was the message; and the message here was mud.

Writing one year after the death of Innis, Marshall McLuhan observed: 'If one were asked to state briefly the basic change which occurred in the thought of Innis in his last decade it could be said that he shifted his attention from the trade-routes of the external world to the trade-routes of the mind.'[16] There was truth in this simplification. Innis had indeed turned to consider different sorts of media, numbered among which were words. And words, like rivers – as in the instance of the word communications – may change their content. But he remained interested in the external world, particularly as it related to the ideological and material structures of empire. And it was precisely here that his late work related most closely to that of other Canadian scholars.

For if, during his lifetime, those scholars tended to be bewildered by, or uninterested in, communications theory, some shared his interest in written and unwritten traditions, at least insofar as they related to the British, American, and Canadian constitutions; and many shared his concerns for the changing forms of empire, at least insofar as they related to the British and Canadian empires. Indeed, in this latter regard, Canadian history was then concerned with little else. Yet if early critics of the late work tended to be blind to the context of the early work, they were no less blind to this wider imperial context of which they, themselves, were a part.

V

During Innis's lifetime, the dominant, non-republican concepts of empire entertained in Canada were those of constitutional historians concerned to trace contemporary forms of government in the British Empire from earlier forms. Taking many of their key ideas from unwritten conventions of parliamentary government and from explanations for the imperial breakdown that had attended the American War of Independence, these scholars were most markedly influenced by the political theory and rhetoric that had attended the mid-nineteenth-century triumph of the Canadian 'Baldwinite' reform movement, the leaders of which derived many ideas and sentiments from eighteenth-century Irish Whigs, or 'Volunteers,' as they termed themselves. These Irish Volunteers had wrested a paper independence for their parliament at Dublin from that at Westminster, and thereafter they had vainly struggled to make that paper independence real. As eighteenth-century mercantile forms of government yielded to nineteenth-century pressures for *laissez-faire*, Canadian Baldwinite reformers sought to apply their Whig ideas, a shifting complex of which became attached to their party slogan: 'Responsible Government and the Voluntary Principle.' By the twentieth century the Irish Whig background had been lost sight of, but 'responsible government,' the idea of which was then thought to have originated in the 1820s and 1830s in Canada, had come to be accepted as a concept of political science, and indeed of constitutional law. Thus in *Baldwin, Lafontaine, Hincks: Responsible Government*, the political economist Stephen Leacock observed that in his own day Robert Baldwin had frequently been derided as a 'man of one idea.' 'Time has shown,' Leacock commented, 'that this "one idea" of Robert Baldwin, – the conception of responsible government, – has proved the corner-stone of the British imperial system.'[17] The term 'responsible government,' however, remained imprecise; for, while it signified the right of colonial legislatures to the practice of ministerial responsibility after the model of unwritten conventions prevailing at Westminster, it was also used to denote what was necessarily implied by this practice, namely complete colonial autonomy. And it was in this latter sense that responsible government was perceived to lie at the heart of a new association of sovereign states that was emerging from older imperial structures, the British Commonwealth of Nations. Thus it became a matter of concern to imperially oriented scholars to establish that this form of autonomy was complementary to, rather than contradictory of, imperial unity.*

It was within this context that Chester Martin published *Empire and Commonwealth: Studies in Governance and Self-Governance in Canada* in 1929. The development of the eighteenth-century empire into the modern commonwealth, Martin argued, was due to the achievement of responsible government, which prevented the empire from being further shattered by the legislative structure of the old empire. Martin, however, was less interested in this than in a continuity of ideas and attitudes from the eighteenth century that he took to be the very cement of empire. As William Kilbourn has put it: 'He harked back with "a melancholy interest" and longing to the undivided North America of the mid-eighteenth century, when Benjamin Franklin called the British Empire the greatest political structure that human wisdom and freedom had ever yet erected, and dared to predict "that the foundations of [its] future grandeur and stability ... lie in America." '[18] This, to be sure, was a nostalgic view of empire; but the point to be noticed is that it was *idealist*.

To others the Commonwealth of Nations seemed little more than the ideological husk of an empire in the last stages of

---

* The material treated in this paragraph is more fully developed in chapter 4. I have also treated aspects of it in 'Whiggery, Nationality and the Upper Canadian Reform Tradition,' *Canadian Historical Review* 56 (1975).

decline. Such was the view of Donald Creighton whose Laurentian thesis was informed by a concept of empire that was *materialist*. Empire, Creighton thought, was dependent upon mercantile systems, upon centralized governments, and upon prescriptive statutes rather than upon parliamentary tradition. Such was the 'commercial empire of the St. Lawrence,' which in extended form became the Dominion of Canada after 1867 but which first existed as an integral part of the British mercantile empire. Because of the struggle for responsible government within the colonies, and the triumph of the free trade movement in Britain, the larger mercantile structure collapsed by the 1850s; but out of its wreckage emerged the expanded empire of the St Lawrence known as the Dominion of Canada.[19]

Of critical importance to any understanding of Creighton is the fact that this new empire very closely resembled the old one, which, in most respects, served as its model. As envisaged in 1867, for example, provinces were to relate to the new federal government very much as colonies had once related to the imperial government in London. The rights to appoint and instruct lieutenant-governors to the provinces, to disallow provincial legislation, to make laws binding upon the provinces, and so forth were given to the central government; and the imperial model was departed from only to strengthen that government. Thus representatives to the federal parliament were to be elected from the provinces, as they had not been from the colonies; the powers of the provinces were specifically defined, as had never been the case with respect to colonial governments; and this whole federal structure was now entrenched in an imperial statute, the British North America Act. And, from an economic point of view, this structure, like the old, was underpinned by a mercantile system, the so-called National Policy of 1878, which was really three interrelated policies of transcontinental railway building, settlement of the western hinterland tapped by this communications system, and a protective tariff calculated to unite that staple-producing region with its eastern manufacturing metropolis. The Conservatives, observed Creighton with respect to these policies, 'had found their answers to the riddle of national unity; and for the next half-dozen years they plunged into a wild career of economic and political nationalism.'[20]

The basic structures of the old empire and the new dominion indeed had much in common; and almost everything Creighton has written may be read as a defence of these forms, or as counter-attacks upon their many enemies. Thus he assailed the *laissez-faire* doctrines of Adam Smith and other classical economists that relaxed the tariff structure of the old empire,[21] even as he assailed the legal doctrine of the justices of the Privy Council who loosened the language of the written Canadian constitution to very nearly the same effect.[22]

Thus Creighton wrote as much from within a tradition as did Martin, for as the latter harked back to the Whig tradition of Baldwinite reform, the former did the same with regard to a Tory tradition of those loyal to a concept of the old united empire. In conflict with each other since the eighteenth century, these two traditions had also been in conflict with a third, which derived its ideology and conceptual models from the American republic that emerged from the imperial breakdown that so concerned the other two.

Essentially oral, all three traditions structured political attitudes, interpretations of past history, and one's understanding of contemporary actuality. The resilience of these traditions in face of fundamental change, and of contradictory or incompatible evidence of a written nature, is illustrated by Chester Martin after he had considered the Laurentian thesis. In this last major work, as Kilbourn has observed, Martin 'went so far as to dismiss economic factors such as "Western oil, Quebec iron, the St. Lawrence seaway, prolific industrial expansion" as "the more specious aspects of nationhood." '[23]

VI

These conflicting traditions, with their varying concepts of empire, afford a context against which *Empire and Communications* and other late work may be usefully understood. Innis differed from the Whig school of Martin in that he regarded 'the struggle for responsible government' as 'essentially a struggle for jobs for the native born,'[24] and more especially in that he did not treat economic factors as specious aspects of either empire or 'nationhood.' But because of his mistrust of written constitutions, and because of a related regard for the principles of *laissez-faire*, he seems to have been also strongly opposed to the Tory tradition of Creighton.

The economist W.T. Easterbrook once remarked that Innis 'remained throughout [his career] a disciple of Adam Smith and no name appears more frequently in his observations on economics past and present.'[25] Like Smith, Innis was hostile to monopolies of power; but, beyond this, he was opposed to the means whereby such power was entrenched and structures of government made resistant to change that necessarily attended shifts in the balance of power. It was not statutory prescription, he contended, but the flexible traditions of the common law that enabled the British constitution to adapt itself to such radical change in the nineteenth century;[26] and it was in like fashion that he reflected upon the federal structure of Canada. 'The British North America Act,' he wrote, 'has produced its own group of idolators and much has been done to interpret the views and sayings of the fathers of Confederation in a substantial body of patristic literature. But though interpretations of decisions of the Privy Council have been subjected to intensive study and complaints have been made about their inconsistency, inconsistencies have implied flexibility and have offset the dangers of rigidity characteristic of written constitutions.'[27] 'Freedom in Canada,' he wrote elsewhere, 'rests on the tenuous support of the Privy Council and on continued struggle between the provinces and the Dominion ... The lack of unity which has preserved Canadian unity threatens to disappear.'[28] Views of this sort were entirely contradictory of the centralist bias and constitutional understanding that informed the Laurentian thesis as expounded by Creighton.

Yet the materialist-idealist conflict, which we have noticed with regard to the traditions of Creighton and Martin, informed also the imperial theory of Innis. Just as he had once perceived that the shift in the material culture of the Indians occasioned by the fur trade had transformed or destroyed those societies, so too he thought that a shift in the material culture of Europe occasioned by the Industrial Revolution, and the ideas this generated, constituted a threat to civilization and the empires that sustained it. It was here that he departed both from Adam Smith and from basic assumptions that sustained Creighton's concept of empire. 'An interest in material goods,' he wrote, 'which characterized the Scottish people, represented notably in Adam Smith, has been followed by an attitude described by Samuel Butler: "All progress is based upon a universal innate desire on the part of every organism to live beyond its income." The concern with specialization and excess, making more and better mousetraps, precludes the possibility of understanding a preceding civilization concerned with balance and proportion.'[29]

Certainly it precluded the possibility of understanding Innis, whose concern for balance and proportion was at odds with what he took to be an undue materialist bias in both historical explanation and its social context. Here he claimed to stand with John Maynard Keynes who, asserting 'that he belonged to the first generation to throw hedonism out the window and to escape from the Benthamite tradition,' had contended that the calculus of interest was 'the worm which has been gnawing at the insides of modern civilisation and is responsible for its pres-

ent moral decay.' It was this escape from the Benthamite calculus, according to Keynes, that had 'served to protect the whole
lot of us from the final *reductio ad absurdum* of Benthamism
known as Marxism.'[30]

But Innis was not *entirely* opposed to Marxism. Indeed, in
defending what he termed 'the living tradition, which is peculiar
to the oral as against the mechanized tradition,' he once
remarked: 'Much of this will smack of Marxian interpretation
but I have tried to use the Marxian interpretation to interpret
Marx. There has been no systematic pushing of the Marxian
conclusion to its ultimate limit, and in pushing it to its limit,
showing its limitations.'[31] Yet in many ways the late work of
Innis seems to have been just that. It was Marx, not Innis, after
all, who first taught that the fundamental and determining
factor in all societies was the mode of economic production, that
all important changes in the culture of a period were ultimately
to be explained in terms of changes in the economic substruc-
ture. What Innis had to say about the effects of staple production
in staple-producing societies was in no way contradictory of this
doctrine and, in all probability, owed much to it. But in his late
work he seems to have pushed this doctrine to its limits by
treating such interrelated media of communication as language,
writing, and printing not only as technologies that disrupted
and transformed societies at an economic level, but also as media
that, by a process of mental conditioning, altered the human
psyche by imposing literal-mindedness and linear patterns of
thought. Linear concepts of time, and related linear concepts
of historical development, Innis suggested, were a product of
this technological conditioning.

Innis might have pushed this doctrine yet further by propos-
ing that what one technology had accomplished, new, or other,
technologies yet might serve to undo or alter. But he never did;
that was the work of McLuhan. Instead he insisted that written

and oral traditions be held *in balance*. This was one of the least impressive aspects of his thought in that it boiled down to a proposal for a sort of stasis in a world in which, as he himself pointed out, all things were subject to change.

VII

In this chapter it has been suggested that the late work of Innis may be usefully understood if referred back to its matrix, back to that land of crumbling empires and of scrambled signals that was Canada. And it has also been suggested that it be referred to the more immediate matrix of the mind that generated it, to a mind reflected by literary style.

What Innis wrote was never drafted with the rigid precision of a written constitution nor did it always conform to the more flexible standards of conventional scholarly reporting. Indeed some of his more idiosyncratic prose has suggested to Carl Berger 'a mind caught up in kind of intellectual cyclone where everything impinged all at once and from all directions, and where there seemed to be no place for stability and contemplation.'[32] The mind of Innis might well thus appear to have been simply distracted.

But one must remember that Innis had come to regard normative literary forms as so many fetters of the mind. And it must also be remembered that events and ideas do impinge all at once and from all directions in living reality as they do not, and cannot, in written prose of a logical and sequentially ordered nature. Writing, Innis observed, 'implied a decline in the power of expression and the creation of grooves which determined the channels of thought of readers and later writers.'[33]

This may well partly explain why he thought and wrote as he did. It is perhaps the reason his stylistic peculiarities bear some resemblance to the 'McLuhanese' employed by the leading interpreter of his late work. Understood in terms of itself, and not judged by way of preconceived thought patterns, the prose of Innis, like that of McLuhan, can serve to jolt one's thought from the grooves and channels to which it has long been habituated. This is a matter to be pursued further in the following chapters.

TWO

McLUHAN
AND OTHERS
ON INNIS

I

Harold Innis was once thought to be a careful, thorough scholar
of penetrating insight, a thinker of monumental importance in
the historiography of Canada. 'Innis succeeded more than any
other writer of the twentieth century,' observed Donald
Creighton, 'in giving both breadth and depth to Canadian studies in history and the social sciences.'[1] But Innis was also thought
to be a quite incompetent writer of English prose.

When in 1937 he submitted the manuscript of *The Cod Fisheries* (1940) to James T. Shotwell, general editor of the Carnegie
series 'Canada and the United States,' Shotwell congratulated
him upon having made 'a fundamental contribution to our
knowledge' but noticed that his work was far from being ready
for publication. Again as Creighton put it, 'Innis was at his most
ineffectual in the final stages of the preparation of a manuscript.'

His style was difficult, highly condensed, extremely elliptical, and not
infrequently obscure. Long, none too obviously relevant quotations
and big chunks of statistics were inserted, in a solidly unassimilated
form, in the middle of his text. The steps which had led him from the
immense detail of his evidence to the grand, sweeping generalizations
of his conclusion were often most imperfectly indicated; and there were
huge excrescences in the material and gaps and discontinuities in
the argument which might only too easily bewilder and exasperate a
reader. It had been true within limits ... of all his writings. It was
perhaps more apparent in this volume, which was the largest he had
ever produced.[2]

Creighton here had regard only to what Innis had written
before 1940; but few critics were of the opinion that his literary
ability improved with time and experience.

To the contrary, to most critics his writing seemed to have
worsened; and his scholarly methodology with it. The essays

that he published in *The Bias of Communication* (1951), for example, received a scathing review from E.R. Adair, who was
remembered by his admiring student W.J. Eccles as a historian
of high standards given to harsh criticism and a man with a
complete inability to suffer fools or frauds gladly.[3] Of Innis's
essays Adair observed:

> It is doubtful if any reader will rise from their perusal with a feeling of
> much satisfaction, for these papers have serious defects. They suffer
> from endless repetitions of the same evidence, often in almost the same
> words ... They are utterly lacking in historical proportion ... Mr. Innis
> is not an expert in ancient or mediaeval history; it is true that he has
> consulted numerous authorities, as his many references show ... Too
> often, however, Mr. Innis takes ... [their] conclusions ... boils them
> down to single statements, and so presents ... what is at the best a mere
> series of half-truths.[4]

'To add to the reader's bewilderment,' added Adair, 'there is
also Mr. Innis's rather unfortunate literary style; he rarely trou-
bles to put in the words, let alone the phrases, that would show
what connection there was in his mind between a sentence and
the ones that precede and follow it, thus leaving to the reader
the task of interpreting this form of intellectual shorthand.'

In at least one respect Adair was quite mistaken. One reader,
Marshall McLuhan, arose from a perusal of Innis's essays with
great satisfaction, indeed with great excitement and interest.
The lack of connection between sentences and the intellectual
shorthand involving the reader in interpretation that so irritated Adair the historian fascinated this literary critic. There
was a resemblance, McLuhan would contend, between the style
of Innis and that of the modernists.

Innis knew little or nothing of this school of experimental
painters, poets, novelists, and composers of music; and this was
well understood by McLuhan. He therefore speculated that

Innis had stumbled upon modernist techniques more or less by accident. As was noticed in the previous chapter, the world of the media, as viewed by Innis, was a place of complex dialectical oppositions. In the modern world, in technologically advanced countries, particularly in the United States, this dialectic appeared to him to be hastening to a resolution of catastrophe. But Innis, McLuhan suggested, hesitated to draw this fearful conclusion. 'He created a stammer in his mind and in his prose to protect the sensibilities of his audience.'[5] And as a liberal, McLuhan would suggest elsewhere, Innis was torn between his trust in the blessings of industry and his awareness of the power of the historic process to undo everything it seemed to have achieved. 'His prose took on the staccato note of alarm and haste. Much of the "obscurity" of his later writing was perhaps an effort to hide even from himself the growing pessimism about the trends which were anything but obscure to him.'[6]

These were interesting speculations. They proceeded, however, from the belief McLuhan shared with other scholars that Innis fundamentally changed his thinking and his writing late in life. If, as was contended in the last chapter, this was not the case, these hypotheses would seem to be not well founded. In any event they are unnecessary to our further argument. Much more important was McLuhan's identification of Innis's style with that of the modernists and his suggestion that it was related to problems of discovery and explanation.

McLuhan read the late work of Innis the way he read 'The Love Song of J. Alfred Prufrock.' 'For anyone acquainted with poetry since Baudelaire and with painting since Cézanne,' he declared, 'the later world of Harold A. Innis is quite readily intelligible. He brought their kinds of contemporary awareness of the electric age to organize the data of the historian and the social scientist. Without having studied modern art and poetry, he yet discovered how to arrange his insights in patterns that nearly resemble the art forms of our time.' 'Innis,' he contended, 'presents his insights in a mosaic structure of *seemingly* [emphasis mine] unrelated and disproportioned sentences and aphorisms.'[7]

As indicated by both Creighton and Adair, there was certainly a lack of logical connection between many of Innis's sentences; but neither of these critics suspected that there might be a parallel lack of connection between ideas in Innis's own mind. As they saw it he was simply unable to give proper expression to connections he himself was well aware of. But, if McLuhan were correct, important *relationships*, quite other than logical *connections*, obtained between and among the ideas of Innis. McLuhan tended to think, however, that Innis had consciously contrived the form in which he had cast his ideas. Perhaps at the back of his mind was the manner in which new forms had been consciously contrived by Stravinski or Picasso or other of the modernists.

But Innis, himself, seems to have been remarkably unconscious of what he was doing. In the spring of 1952, when he was dying of cancer, the economist W.T. Easterbrook wrote to him about his own 'current preoccupation with McLuhan's "juxtaposition of unlikes"' as a means of gaining new insights into what is juxtaposed. 'It is a method not at all uncommon in your own writings but it is only recently that I have begun to see its possibilities. It is the only way I know out of the dilemma of narrative versus "scientific" history.'[8] 'I agree with you,' replied Innis, 'about the importance of juxtaposition along the lines suggested by McLuhan. It seems to offer the only prospect of escape from the obsession of one's own culture, but of course needs to be carefully considered since while one's own views of one's own culture change as a result of looking at other cultures nevertheless the problem of objectivity always seems to emerge.'[9]

This curious reply was almost completely tangential to Easterbrook's query. Referring not at all to his own use of the technique, Innis appeared to be suggesting that the discovery of the usefulness of juxtaposing ideas was not his but McLuhan's. His letter further suggests that he very imperfectly understood Easterbrook. For the 'juxtaposition of unlikes' that was the latter's explanation of the technique is not the same thing as the juxtaposition of cultures to escape from personal bias that Innis had in mind. And this, in turn, would seem to have little or nothing to do with the dilemma of narrative versus 'scientific' history that was the concern of Easterbrook.

It is significant that what Innis appears to have had in mind was not what Easterbrook had just written to him but some somewhat different reflections upon the juxtaposition of unlikes that McLuhan had earlier expounded in *The Mechanical Bride* (1951). We shall return to a consideration of the influence of this book further below; and we shall also return to the argument that what Easterbrook referred to as 'a method not at all uncommon in your own writings' was really patterns of ideas existing in Innis's mind. But here it should be remarked that few things are more difficult than to perceive the structure of one's own thought; and Innis appears to have been unconscious of the pattern of his.

McLuhan began to read the late work only after he was made curious by learning that *The Mechanical Bride* had been placed on the reading list of one of Innis's courses in political economy. Then, almost but not quite accepting the current view that upon writing *Empire and Communications* Innis had departed radically from earlier methods and interests, he suggested that he had abandoned an early procedure of 'working with a "point of view" ' or perspective to 'that of the generating of insights by the method of "interface", as it is named in chemistry. "Interface" refers to the interaction of substances in a kind of mutual irritation. In art and poetry this is precisely the technique of "symbolism" (Greek "symballein" – to throw together) with its paratactic procedure of juxtaposing without connectives.'[10]

McLuhan here was thinking of juxtapositions of the sort to be found in 'Minerva's Owl': 'Alexandria broke the link between science and philosophy. The library was an imperial instrument to offset the influence of Egyptian priesthood.'[11]

Certainly McLuhan seems to have discovered the only possible way of making sense out of writings that simply maddened other readers. To search for logical connection, or to try to impose it, in some of Innis's work is a completely futile enterprise leading only to frustration of mind and of purpose. But McLuhan was mistaken in thinking that Innis's discontinuous modes of thought were only arrived at late in his career. Creighton and other critics detected them in the early work. They are less evident there, however, than they later became. Part of the problem, it would seem, is that Innis initially made more of an effort to write in a conventional fashion than he did towards the end of his life. But, beyond this, his early work received editorial attention that unquestionably removed much that was distinctively his own.

Compare, for example, the attention given to the notorious *Cod Fisheries* manuscript with that afforded *Empire and Communications*. 'Shotwell,' wrote Creighton, 'tentatively suggested an editorial assistant; and Innis accepted the proposal. Arthur E. McFarlane ... an admirer of Innis's work, and a writer who had considerable experience in preparing manuscript for the press, came up to Toronto [from New York] to lend his assistance; and, during the winter of 1938, he and Innis began, in collaboration, a thorough revision of the *Cod Fisheries*.'[12] Thus this manuscript received unusually close editorial attention. By way of contrast Innis felt obliged to apologize for numerous errors in spelling in *Empire and Communications*. The difficulty, he explained, 'is in part due to publication overseas and the slips of proof readers in the Oxford Press.'[13] One can but speculate as to the outcome if this latter work had received the attention of McFarlane; but the difference would surely have been considerable. One must also remember that all the rest of the late work consisted of articles republished in book form. By their very nature these books would have been even less subject to editorial alteration.

Much further light has been cast on these problems by the posthumous publication of Innis's 'Idea File,' a work that only became generally available in 1980, the year of McLuhan's own death. Never intended for publication in this form, this file, if not revealing the quintessential Innis, does show, at least, the unrewritten, unedited positioning of ideas as they passed through his mind. Consider this entry:

Rise of mysticism with clash of one group of symbols with another, i.e. simplifying scriptures and scholastic philosophy for German nuns led to mysticism. Developed concepts difficult to get into simpler language – Latin abstractions into German or Greek into Latin – philosophy versus law – missionaries teaching hell to Eskimos. Impact of science and scientific thought on humanities produces social sciences or form of mysticism. But also makes for inventions and abstraction. Newton dynamics – American constitution. Darwin's evolution on social sciences. Hardness of scientific thought produces fuzziness at points encroaching on humanities. Limits of education as device to reduce gap between illiterary [sic] and abstractions of learned language – emphasized symbols of Middle Ages.[14]

After Innis's death a committee consisting of his wife, Mary Quayle Innis, his son Donald, Professors Donald Creighton and W.T. Easterbrook, and the sociologist Professor S.D. Clark decided that the 'Idea File' was unpublishable. 'Given his cryptic style of writing,' observed Clark, 'and his tendency to make great leaps in his thinking, there was clearly no way these notes could be prepared for publication.'[15]

Had E.R. Adair read the stream of consciousness quoted above, he might well have concluded that Innis had taken final leave of his scholarly senses. Had McLuhan read it, the abrupt juxtapositions and transitions of thought might have reminded him of the mosaic structure of T.S. Eliot's *The Waste Land*, to which indeed there would seem to be some resemblance. He might also have recalled the movements of the mind of Leopold Bloom as he wandered through the streets of Dublin in James Joyce's *Ulysses*.

In any event Innis was musing upon the passage of ideas from one medium or frame of reference to another and upon the resulting transformations and consequences. He did not do so by logical connection but by way of analogy; and not from a diachronic perspective but synchronically. Thus he perceived that the experience of pagan 'Eskimos' acquiring concepts of hell from European Christian missionaries in some ways paralleled the experience of medieval German-speaking nuns acquiring information translated from Latin and Greek. There was no logical or necessarily sequential connection here; but in the mind of Innis there was an analogical relationship. He was engaged in 'pattern recognition.'

The 'Idea File' establishes that McLuhan was essentially right about Innis's odd prose. But it also shows how closely that prose was related to the private musings of its author's mind. It is additional evidence, in short, that discontinuous prose was not a technique Innis had to discover; it was a mirror image of the way he normally thought. And it is Innis's discontinuous, analogical cast of mind that bridges the alleged dichotomy separating his early work from what came later.

In the introduction to *Empire and Communications* Innis remarked that 'the subject of communication offers possibilities in that it occupies a crucial position in the organization and administration of government and in turn of empires and of Western civilization.' He further remarked that he had been led 'to give particular attention to this subject' by his studies of the river systems of North America, particularly that of the St

Lawrence.[16] Students of Innis's thought, however, have paid little or no attention to this assertion. They have rather tended to think that he was led directly to his late interests by his studies of the pulp and paper industries that immediately preceded them. The mind of Innis was not that linearly sequential. Certainly he was influenced by his pulp and paper studies; but, as argued in the previous chapter, the key to understanding the relationship obtaining between his early and late work is *The Fur Trade in Canada*.

We have already seen how in *Empire and Communications* Innis's treatment of the content of the river Nile – silt – parallels his earlier treatment of the commercial content of the St Lawrence – fur, timber, and wheat. In both instances these basic staples structured and otherwise influenced the communities dependent upon them. They did so, moreover, in ways that resemble the manner in which he thought of the technologies of writing and printing as affecting society. As McLuhan would remark, Innis was very conscious of the hidden and revolutionary effects of the supercession of one medium of communication by another; the loss to the Roman Empire, for example, of its source of supply of papyrus and the supercession of papyrus by parchment subjected that empire to stress and structural change. This was very much after the fashion in which Innis had earlier treated beaver pelts and their supercession in the commerce of the St Lawrence. The birch-bark canoe was an admirable medium of communication for shipping furs from the far west to Montreal; but it was entirely inadequate to the demands of the later commodities, timber and grain. New commodities begot new technologies – canal building around rapids, the construction of railroads to markets and sources of supply untapped by waterways – that were revolutionary in their implications. 'Each staple in its turn left its stamp,' wrote Innis of this Canadian model, 'and the shift to new staples invariably produced periods of crisis in which adjustments in the old structure were painfully made and a new pattern created in relation to a new staple.'[17] In the late work Innis wrote much the same thing with respect to shifts from an oral tradition to a written technology, to that of print, to that of radio, and so forth. Staple commodities, of course, were not technologies; but both could be thought of as media of communication, and both could have similar effects.

McLuhan, who knew relatively little of the history and historiography of Canada, seems not to have noticed these parallels. They could not be noticed by anyone, however, were Innis not read in the manner McLuhan indicated.

II

McLuhan read Innis the way he did by reason of an earlier interest in the relation of art forms to the models of physicists, and of both of these to social structures. Long before encountering Innis he had written: 'Ever since Burckhardt saw that the meaning of Machiavelli's method was to turn the state into a work of art by the rational manipulation of power, it has been an open possibility to apply the method of art analysis to the critical evaluation of society.'[18] He had also referred to the layout of a newspaper page as a symbolist landscape, and had discerned the techniques of discontinuity in the work of contemporary historians and anthropologists. 'Discontinuity,' he had written, 'is in different ways a basic concept both of quantum and relativity physics. It is the way in which a Toynbee looks at civilizations, or a Margaret Mead at human cultures. Notoriously, it is the visual technique of a Picasso, the literary technique of James Joyce.'[19] In short, discontinuity was a unifying technique common to a wide variety of disciplines usually imagined to have little or nothing in common. But what then was so special about Innis; what distinguished him from a Toynbee or a Mead?

Toynbee, as a comparative historian, made all civilizations

contemporary with his own; that is to say, he took a synchronic as opposed to a diachronic view of the past. 'The past is immediately available as a working model for present political experiment.' Mead's *Male and Female*, McLuhan further explained, illustrated a similar method; 'The cultural patterns of several societies, quite unrelated to one another or to our own, are abruptly overlayered in cubist or Picasso style to provide a greatly enriched image of human potentialities. By this method the greatest possible detachment from our own immediate problems is achieved. The voice of reason is audible only to the detached observer.'[20] (It was this method of achieving 'the greatest possible detachment,' it would appear, that Innis had in mind in making his strange reply to Easterbrook.)

In McLuhan's opinion Innis went well beyond anything to be discovered in Toynbee or Mead. This was partly by reason of his condensed, aphoristic, paratactic prose. 'I think there are lines appearing in Empire and Communications,' McLuhan privately told him, 'which suggest the possibility of organizing an entire school of studies ...'* But beyond Innis's own writing, McLuhan was fascinated by what he had to say about writing in general.

As noted in the last chapter, Innis held that the ideal content of a material medium of communication was to a large extent determined by the nature of that material medium – the nature of a message inscribed on a clay tablet, for example, being quite different from that printed in a newspaper. Being relatively biased with respect to either time or space, media gave a corres-

---

* Marshall McLuhan to [Harold] Innis, 14 Mar. [19]51. The original of this document appears to have been lost or misplaced in the Innis Papers at the University of Toronto Archives. Fortunately McLuhan, apparently realizing its importance, had it copied in 1976. This copy is in the McLuhan Papers in the National Archives at Ottawa. The letter has been printed in Matie Molinaro, Corinne McLuhan, and William Toye, eds, *Letters of Marshall McLuhan* (Toronto, Oxford, New York 1987).

ponding bias to institutions dependent upon them, papyrus, for example, making it possible for the Roman Empire to communicate over space in a way that was impossible for the Babylonian Empire, which was dependent upon clay. It was therefore possible for the Roman Empire to be more highly centralized and to exercise more extended control than the Babylonian.

But media of communication, according to Innis, also had psychic effects upon users. The invention of writing made readers less dependent upon memory than the illiterate and led to the organization of ideas into new, hitherto impossible, structures. And writing, and more especially printing, led to a tendency to order ideas in linearly sequential patterns that made for 'literal' mindedness and blocked figurative perception. These technological effects of the medium were examined by McLuhan in *The Gutenburg Galaxy* (1962), which he was pleased to think of as 'a footnote to the observations of Innis on the subject of the psychic and social consequences, first of writing and then of printing.'[21]

Writing, printing, and other media studied by Innis related the interior world of the mind to the external world of technology and institutions; and this became a peculiar interest of McLuhan.* Writing privately he observed:

---

* An important argument to the contrary has been made by James W. Carey. In seeking to distinguish between the work of Innis and McLuhan he has contended that the latter departed from the work of the former by placing a much greater emphasis upon the psychic consequences of the media ('Harold Adams Innis and Marshall McLuhan,' *Antioch Review* [Spring 1967]).

'The question I am asking,' he wrote, 'is this: What is absolutely central to the Innis argument and how does it compare to the central notion in McLuhan's work? Although McLuhan has occasionally characterized his work as an extension of Innis', I want to suggest that McLuhan has taken a relatively minor but recurring theme of Innis' work ... and made it central to his entire argument. Conversely, McLuhan has neglected or ignored the principal argument developed by Innis' (15). Both McLuhan and Innis,

Although the church began and continues, with a communication theory or doctrine, Western philosophy has had none since the Greeks. That is, in Western philosophy I have been able to find no doctrine of the changes which man inflicts upon his entire psyche by his own artifacts. The Old Testament is full of awareness of these changes, which St. Paul, 1 Romans i, calls 'vain imaginings' etc. ... Until the work of Harold Innis I have been unable to discover any epistemology of experience as opposed to epistemology of knowledge. I can find no

---

he contended, assume the centrality of communications technology; but they differ as to the effects they see deriving from it. 'Whereas Innis sees communication technology principally affecting social organization, McLuhan sees its principal effect on sensory organization and thought. McLuhan has much to say about perception and thought but little about institutions; Innis says much about institutions and little about perception and thought.'

These dichotomies are unreal. Innis, like other historians treating the rise and fall of civilizations, paid a great deal of attention to institutions. What is extraordinary is that in doing so he also paid attention to perception and thought. It was here that he was perhaps at his most original. That he made only passing references to them means nothing; for it was characteristic of the man to make only passing references to things he regarded as of central importance. We have noted that he made only a passing reference to his early work in *Empire and Communications*; and we have noted also how that has misled many critics. This characteristic and the importance he assigned to the effects of writing upon the mind will be made evident later in this chapter. McLuhan, on the other hand, paid more attention to institutions than Carey allowed. This is revealed in Part 2 of *Understanding Media: The Extensions of Man* (1964) and more obviously in books like *Take Today: The Executive as Dropout* (1972), which was published after Carey wrote.

In considering Innis and McLuhan in relation to institutions, moreover, Carey ignored language. Since the time of Ferdinand de Saussure language has been regarded as perhaps the most basic of the institutions of mankind. The structure of language, it has been contended by the anthropologist Claude Lévi-Strauss, parallels that of basic social organization. It is difficult to imagine anything more central to the thought of both Innis and McLuhan than language, the technology that lay behind both writing and printing.

doctrine of how and why men are changed in their inner natures by their own technologies. Hegel merely passes the buck to the cosmos in this matter.[22]

How and why men are changed in their inner natures by their technologies was one of McLuhan's leading interests; but he was also interested in Innis's views on the impact of technology on institutions and social structures.

'Harold Innis,' he maintained, 'was the first person to hit upon the *process* of change as implicit in the *forms* of media technology.'[23] McLuhan called this 'formal causality.' 'It need no longer seem strange,' he wrote, 'that peoples like the Greeks and Romans, who had experienced the alphabet, should also have been driven in the direction of conquest and organization-at-a-distance.' Innis, he added, also explained 'why print causes nationalism and not tribalism; and why print causes price systems and markets such as cannot exist without print.'[24] And Innis, he declared, 'had hit upon the means of using history as the physicist uses the cloud chamber. By bouncing the unknown form against known forms, he discovered the nature of new or little known form.'[25] But since Innis was bouncing not particles but ideas, and these not in a cloud chamber but in his own mind, we are concerned once more with the forms of thought.

What Innis and McLuhan perhaps had most in common was an uncommon ability to perceive structure, to distinguish form from content, and to observe one form in relation to other forms. Innis seems to have done this instinctively, and probably not altogether consciously. McLuhan, on the other hand, was highly conscious of this activity and wrote of it at length. The necessity of distinguishing form from content underlay his famous slogan 'the medium is the message,' which, contrary to the opinion of many, did not mean that content is of no importance. It meant rather that content itself should be thought of as form, the content of any medium being always another medium. 'The content of writing is speech, just as the

written word is the content of print, and print is the content of
the telegraph. If it is asked "What is the content of speech?", it
is necessary to say, "It is an actual process of thought, which is
in itself nonverbal." '[26] If a non-verbal process of thought is the
content of speech, which, in turn, is the content of writing, we
are, of course, back to what governed the writing of Innis or,
for that matter, of anyone else. We are back to studying the way
a medium of communication interacts with its content; and back
to examining the way in which both Innis and McLuhan thought
that writing affected both the mind and society at large.

Apart from distinguishing form from content, McLuhan
attached great importance to figure/ground relationships. And
this non-linear mode of perception he also discovered in the
thought of Innis. Towards the end of *Empire and Communications*,
McLuhan observed, 'Innis speeds up his sequence of figure-
ground flashes almost to that of a cinematic montage. This
acceleration corresponds to the sense of urgency that he felt as
one involved in understanding the present. It is certainly crucial
for the reader of Innis to recognize his method for presenting
the historical process as inseparable from contemporary reality.'[27] In presenting the historical process, or processes, McLuhan continued, Innis was not presenting the reader with a
perspective or point of view. He was presenting a diagnostic
analysis of a complex process. 'He saw that the figure-ground
relation between written and oral is everywhere in a state of
perpetual change.'[28] Where conventional historians had been
content to search for multiple causal relationships, Innis, it
appeared, looked to the more fundamental effects of the shifting
contexts of these relationships. According to McLuhan, he was
well aware of the manner in which figure/ground relationships
can and do reverse themselves, what was figure becoming
ground, and what was ground becoming figure.

Material conditions can quickly reverse the relationships between written and oral so that, where literacy may be the ground of a culture in

one phase, a sudden loss or access of written materials, for example, may cause the literate *ground* suddenly to dwindle to mere *figure*. That is why Innis carefully watches the changing material conditions of cultures since a reversal of figure-ground relations will put an individualist culture overnight into an extreme bureaucratic or hieratic posture ... Innis saw the Greeks as having finally pushed their written tradition into ascendency over the oral and changing their aristocracy into a sprawling Oriental bureaucracy.[29]

Mosaic-like configurations of ideas, then, some patterned into reversible figure/ground relationships, and a tendency to relate these configurations analogically, are the distinguishing characteristics of Innis's mind as perceived by McLuhan.

III

Over the years historians of Canada have tended to separate very sharply the late work of Innis – that which began with and followed the writing of *Empire and Communications* (1950) – from his early work. As Carl Berger has put it, the later preoccupations of Innis had little direct impact on the writing of Canadian history, and historians 'continued to regard the staples thesis as his major contribution to Canadian studies and were hesitant about accepting his speculations on communications as anything more than exploratory and suggestive beginnings.'[30] Although such was indeed the case, this involved denying, or refusing to perceive that 'communications' had anything to do with 'the staples thesis.' And this was to adopt a very strange and significant posture in that, when thinking about this matter in a different context, Canadian historians well knew that underlying Innis's ideas about staple commodities were others clearly related to communications. These notions, somewhat reorganized and reapplied by Donald Creighton in *The Commercial Empire of the St. Lawrence, 1760–1850* (1937), had become celebrated in historical circles as 'the Laurentian thesis.' This term referred to the fundamental importance assigned by both Innis and Creighton to the St Lawrence–Great Lakes communications system. And it is not without interest that inasmuch as both Innis and Creighton thought of this system as being of greater significance than any of its immediate commercial content – first furs, which were succeeded by timber, and then by wheat and flour – they were both contending that 'the medium is the message,' albeit quite unknown to themselves.

Although McLuhan's interest in Innis found its focus in the late work, he did comment very briefly on what preceded it. The later Innis who dominates *The Bias of Communication*, he observed, 'had set out on a quest for the causes of change,' while the early Innis of *The Fur Trade in Canada* had 'conformed a good deal to the conventional patterns of merely reporting and narrating change.'[31] But he did not think that Innis conformed completely. In the concluding chapter of *The Fur Trade*, McLuhan added, Innis did 'venture to interlace or link complex events in a way that reveals the causal processes of change.' He did not precisely indicate, however, just where and how Innis did this.

From the point of view of many historians of Canada, the early Innis was much less of a conventional scholar than McLuhan's brief comment suggests. Such certainly has been the opinion of W.J. Eccles, once a student of Innis's critic, E.R. Adair, and today the leading English-Canadian authority upon the French régime in Canada. In 1979, writing very much in the tradition of his master, Eccles published 'A Belated Review of Harold Adams Innis, *The Fur Trade in Canada*,'[32] a closely argued critique some twenty-three pages in length.

Eccles acknowledged that *The Fur Trade* had been a very influential book indeed; but this he deplored. In his view it was in no way definitive, being rather a carelessly written, slipshod piece of scholarship. 'Unfortunately,' wrote Eccles, 'neither ...

[Innis's] premises, both stated and unstated, his use of historical evidence, nor the conclusions drawn will stand up to close scrutiny and all too many erroneous interpretations of North American history have been made in consequence.'[33] 'The work,' he further contended, 'contains a great mass of information, much of it presented in chapters that lack cohesion, and frequently the evidence presented contradicts the book's conclusions,' but its fundamental flaw was 'that Innis manifestly approached the subject with certain *a priori* premises and conclusions already formed and he chose to disregard any evidence that pointed to different conclusions.'[34]

This expert, detailed criticism is of considerable value to present-day students of the fur trade, particularly those more inclined to reason from, than to argue to, a sacred text. It was written, however, some forty-nine years after the book it criticized was published, and after a lifetime of specialized study by both Eccles and other scholars. *The Fur Trade in Canada*, on the other hand, researched, written, and published between 1923 and 1930, was sandwiched in between work on *A History of the Canadian Pacific Railway* and work on *The Cod Fisheries*, and much else. Innis, in other words was a dedicated generalist, a macrohistorian; even as Eccles is a convinced specialist. To judge his work in this fashion is much like judging a useful piece of rough carpentry by the standards of a cabinet maker.

Bringing the expertise of the specialist to bear on the work of a generalist, however, is far from being a useless enterprise. It is here that Eccles's criticism is of great value. But in two respects his approach is misleading. Absent from his belated review is any appreciation of the context of the times within which Innis worked or, as McLuhan might have expressed it, the ground to which *The Fur Trade in Canada* was figure. And, related to this, is the further absence of recognition of what both Innis and others thought was the book's chief importance. 'Fundamentally,' wrote the book's author, 'the civilization of

North America is the civilization of Europe and the interest of this volume is primarily in the effects of a vast new land area on European civilization.'[35] Focusing his attention upon trade in fur, Eccles paid no attention to the effects of a new land area upon the civilization of Europe. Nor did he deal directly with the communications system of the St Lawrence. And these omissions, as will be shown, are more remarkable than a reader unfamiliar with Eccles's own fine work might suppose. Meanwhile, to retrieve the context within which *The Fur Trade* was first read, we must turn to the observations of one who believed himself to have been influenced by it.

'Innis's thematic achievement,' wrote the historian John Bartlet Brebner, 'was grand and unprecedented,'

and it was accompanied by such a far-ranging array of often minute evidence that it compelled surrender to his arguments even where they were irregularly buttressed. His formal documentation could only be described as whimsical and his scholarly apparatus as casual, but every page of his text conducted the reader deep into the problems and opportunities of the men in the field, Indian and European, or of their managers nearer the economic capitals, or of the politicians whose services they tried to evoke. In effect he wove geography, economic history, changing technology, political adaptation, and far more theory than is evident, into such a vivid, variegated, and tough fabric of explanatory exposition that its rough spots and irregularities could be ignored. One felt that he had collected, carded and spun the fibres and that then the artist in him had responded by composing the coherent design that their nature commanded. He was always both the inductive and the deductive thinker.[36]

The book's sweep, he wrote, 'was so thorough that it substituted an economic, geographical theme for the previous political, personal thesis of Canadian development.'[37] 'As western Canadians know and have come to protest,' he added, 'it substantiated the Laurentian hypothesis of Canada's evolution that the geographer Marion I. Newbigin had glimpsed about the same time and had sketched in *Canada: The Great River, the Lands and the Men* (London 1927).'

Brebner, himself a quite orthodox scholar, appreciated that the originality of Innis proceeded from an unorthodox methodology related to peculiar modes of thought. He is of particular interest here in that, independently of McLuhan, he observed in the early work characteristics that resemble those indicated by McLuhan in work that came later, He noted, for example, that Innis perceived historical data arranged in 'patterns of force.' 'Who before him,' Brebner inquired, '... had even speculated, much less learned, about the powerful patterns of force that were composed from the distinct qualities of bank or shore, ship or boat, green or dry, fisheries, on the one hand, and world markets, on the other.'[38] This pattern of force appears elsewhere in the early work. Innis, for example, employed a 'cyclonic model' in economic theory; and Carl Berger has discerned a reflection of this in some of his prose. 'The sense of urgency back of Innis's later apocalyptic pronouncements,' wrote Berger, 'suggests a mind caught up in a kind of intellectual cyclone where everything impinged all at once and from all directions ...'[39] Patterns like these would seem to resemble those non-linear metaphors or models of force – like the vortex and the maelstrom – later employed by McLuhan. They perhaps also have something in common with the moving pattern of particles in the physicist's cloud chamber to which McLuhan likened Innis's method of discovery; and to those patterns in the poetry and painting of symbolists and cubists that he believed foreshadowed the thought of modern physics. Returning to Brebner, however, the point is that he came very close to recognizing that Innis's originality was related to an escape from models of actuality that were linear.

Brebner also suggested that Innis's novel perceptions and

modes of thought tended to be in conflict with, and to block, his powers of literary expression, most notably with respect to the writing of *The Cod Fisheries*. This was 'the most ambitious enterprise in economic history and political economy' he ever undertook, 'for it presented a novel and perhaps unique problem in exposition.'

To realize this, one has only to consider that, whereas the normal study is centripetal and has a natural unity around a core. *The Cod Fisheries*, as its subtitle, *The history of an international economy*, indicates, was centrifugal and amounted to the study of very complicated activities in the North Atlantic Maritime Region and of their equally complicated radiating relationship with the rest of North America, the West Indies, South America, Western Europe, and the Mediterranean.[40]

The form of a book, in short, was inappropriate for giving expression to Innis's overall concept. It cannot be claimed, Brebner added, that Innis found 'any magical artistic formula' to solve his problem, 'but the degree of his success, by sometimes fairly brutal expository means, was far beyond ordinary expectation.' These 'fairly brutal expository means,' it will be recalled, were only achieved with the assistance of an editor dispatched for the purpose from New York. And so Brebner was probably here mistaken. A 'magical artistic formula' did indeed shape the work of Innis; but it needed a McLuhan to detect it elsewhere.

To an extent Brebner agreed with Adair, Creighton, Eccles, and the rest with regard to Innis's style. Except for 'a few careful, even graceful, papers of his last decade,' he could be 'ambiguous, contradictory, enigmatic, elliptical, or careless of technical canons.'[41] He attributed this, in part, to haste, Innis being always a man in a hurry to get on to something new. But he also suspected that it was related to Innis's views on the effects of writing. 'There are reasons for connecting these negligent habits,' he declared, 'with his gradually-revealed mistrust of the meticulously-marshalled written word as fossilization or mechanization of knowledge and thought. For him both must be free and dynamic in time. His faith was in the *Logos*.'[42]

In the final analysis, Brebner read Innis much more after the fashion of McLuhan than after that of Adair. 'Why, then,' he inquired, 'when any prig or purist could convict him of abundant sins, was he read and admired throughout the scholarly world? Why was he intellectually exciting?'[43] Underlying all Innis's accomplishments, Brebner thought there was genius, 'genius in the sense of absolute, untrammeled originality, invention, and leaping insights.'

IV

In contrast to this opinion, let us now return to Eccles's belated review. Eccles's final judgment upon Innis was that 'virtually nothing can be found on the credit side of the ledger ... except that ... *The Fur Trade in Canada* was a pioneering work which brought the Canadian fur trade to the attention of a wide audience.' In relation to this verdict, we shall also return to Innis's contention that 'the civilization of North America is the civilization of Europe and the interest of this volume is primarily in the effects of a vast new land area on European civilization.' And all this will be reflected upon in the light of the communications theory of both Innis and McLuhan.

It was not Innis but Frederick Jackson Turner, the most influential of all the historians of the United States, who was first concerned with the effects of a vast new land mass on European civilization. In the 1890s Turner challenged the doctrines of Herbert Baxter Adams, a historian who taught that all American institutions could be traced back to their 'germs' in the forests of medieval Germany. This notion, which recognized no essential differences between the United States and Europe, offended Turner. His own hypothesis, 'the Frontier theory,' he would later allow, 'was pretty much a *reaction* from that due to my indignation.'[44]

The Turnerian frontier was the westward advancing line that, from the seventeenth century until the late nineteenth, separated settled land from unsettled territory. More largely, however, the term referred to the scantily populated lands adjacent to this line. Here European institutions – and indeed eastern American institutions – were conceived of as being continually broken down, and new, distinctively American institutions were thought of as emerging. The frontier was a harsh, lawless environment, a 'crucible' wherein 'immigrants were Americanized, liberated, and fused into a mixed race, English in neither nationality nor characteristics.'[45] The frontier, wrote Turner, is the line of

most rapid and effective Americanization ... It finds him [the immigrant] a European in dress, industries, tools, modes of travel, and thought. It takes him from the railroad car and puts him in the birch canoe. It strips off the garments of civilization and arrays him in the hunting shirt and the moccasin ... Before long he has gone to planting Indian corn and plowing with a sharp stick; he shouts the war cry and takes the scalp in orthodox Indian fashion. In short, at the frontier the environment is at first too strong for the man. He must accept the conditions which it furnishes, or perish, and so he fits himself into the Indian clearings and follows the Indian trails.[46]

But out of this same environment emerged self-reliance, individualism, and American-style democracy.

Doctrine of this sort had great national appeal in the United States; and, for a time, it appealed also to Canadian historians. Did it not, after all, suggest a new and interesting approach to the *coureur de bois*, *voyageur*, and *habitant* of New France? Indeed, what group of American settlers was more prone than they to have fitted themselves into Indian clearings and to have followed Indian trails? As conceived of by Turner, moreover, the frontier was isolated from the east and at odds with it. Might this not help explain Canadian western movements of protest against the dominance of the metropolitan centres of the east, of the Clear Grit movement in Canada West in the 1850s, of prairie populists in the early decades of this century? But theory of this sort also suggested that the historical experience of Canada was essentially that of the United States. And to some Canadian historians this was as little pleasing as the suggestion that the experience of the United States was essentially that of Europe had been to Turner.

Innis, and after him Creighton and others, argued that by reason of the St Lawrence–Great Lakes communication system, Canada, in contrast to the United States, had been shaped and dominated less by western frontiers than by European and eastern metropolitan centres whose agents and emigrants penetrated the west in search of profit, carrying with them the institutions and culture of Europe.

Remarkably enough, one of the most distinguished scholars of this school is W.J. Eccles. As is indicated by the titles of some of his books – *Canada under Louis XIV* (1964), for example, or *France in America* (1972) – Eccles assigns great importance to European metropolitan influence. This is even more clearly indicated by the contents of *The Canadian Frontier 1534–1760* (1969), which he published as one volume in the eighteen-volume series 'Histories of the American Frontier.' This book, moreover, well reveals how remote Eccles is from Turner and how very close to Innis.

The frontier – which, it will be recalled, Turner conceived of as a crucible melting down the cultures of Europe – is defined by Eccles as 'the outer limits of European civilization.'[47] But he also explains that in New France it is possible to distinguish four types of frontier: commercial, religious, settlement, and military; and here he seems to be writing less about a line than about an interface. 'If the Anglo-American frontier is accepted

as the norm,' he contends, 'then Canada can hardly be said to
have had a frontier at all. Rather, it can be said to have been a
metropolis, dominating the hinterland around it ...'[48] And this
he accounts for in terms of communications. 'The St. Lawrence
and Ottawa rivers and the Great Lakes gave the Canadians easy
and direct access to the interior of the continent ... Rivers by
themselves, however, are not enough. A means of transportation is required; and here again the Canadians had a marked
advantage ... The Indian's birchbark canoe was capable of carrying heavy loads, was light enough to be carried around river
obstructions ... and was manufactured entirely from materials
readily available in the Canadian forest.'[49]

This is pure, unadulterated Innis. It is the sort of thing he
thought *The Fur Trade in Canada* was chiefly about. Eccles elaborated these ideas beyond anything contemplated by Innis; but
this much, at least, is almost identical with the conclusions of a
book he discovered to be without redeeming merit beyond
having directed the attention of other scholars to the fur trade.
This much, moreover, is fundamental to Eccles's own theoretical
approach to the history of New France.

Here we are dealing with shifting figure/ground relationships. By the time Eccles wrote his belated review these ideas
had become generally accepted among the historians of Canada.
And they seem to have become so integrated with Eccles's own
ideas that in considering *The Fur Trade in Canada* he was completely unaware of them. In this context these ideas were simply
orthodox, and commonplace – if not old hat. But in another
context, when he was reflecting upon the doctrines of Frederick
Jackson Turner, they were very much before his mind.

V

The late work of Innis, and what McLuhan made of it, have
generally been thought to be irrelevant to the writing of Canadian history. A study of staple commodities, scholars have sup-

posed, could have nothing to do with the history of ideas. It is all somewhat reminiscent of Eskimos acquiring, or not acquiring, concepts of hell from European missionaries. We are dealing, in other words, with the transfer, or lack of transfer, of ideas from one mentality to another. But we are still dealing with transportation, a form of communications that both Innis and McLuhan related to the communication of ideas at both literal and figurative levels of meaning. We are also dealing with the effects of words.

Metaphor, as McLuhan frequently pointed out, is a form of transportation. It comes from the Greek *metapherein*, meaning to carry across. The metaphor of the crucible, as employed by Frederick Jackson Turner, transferred certain historical data previously organized by the metaphor of European germs developing in an American environment to a different pattern of explanation wherein they were reorganized with new data. The concept of the crucible, moreover, was subsumed by Turner's larger notion of the frontier, which at times also functioned as a metaphor and which was associated with a powerful myth, the myth being related to what was conceived to be the traditional American way of life. As late as the 1960s this myth was successfully evoked in the United States by the 'new frontiersmen' of the Kennedy administration and by the 'new frontier' of outer space.

In Canada, as we have seen, these ideas collided with those of Innis. This collision is to be observed in part in *The Canadian Frontier* of W.J. Eccles. In the words of Roy Allen Billington, the leading American authority upon the school of Turner, Eccles here 'grapples successfully with an unsolved problem: did immigrants from the distinctive culture of France respond to the New World environment as did the small farmers of the New England or Virginia back country of that day?'[50] Eccles's answers, Billington found, would 'both please and displease advocates of the theories of Frederick Jackson Turner.' The

seigneurs and *habitants* of New France 'did develop some characteristics typical of Anglo-Americans subjected to the frontier's
influence ... but they failed to develop many others, while their
institutions remained virtually unchanged.'

But this same book, Eccles himself somewhat oddly observed,
'does not attempt to confirm or refute the Turner thesis,'[51] an
assertion that does not make it easy to understand why those
Turnerians alluded to by Billington should be either pleased or
displeased with its findings. According to Eccles, his study
sought rather 'to define the term frontier in the Canadian context.' This simply means he was engaged in emptying the
expression of Turnerian meaning and informing it with his own
Canadian content; and this, in a Canadian context, would seem
to amount to an overthrow of Turner.

But the collision of the ideas of Turner and Innis looms more
largely in the history of ideas in Canada than this single instance
suggests. And in interpreting this conflict the communications
theory of McLuhan is more useful than that of Innis.

Innis, as Brebner observed, was wary of words, particularly
of their written and printed forms, which he believed fossilized
or mechanized knowledge. He mistrusted in particular written
constitutions, which he believed were ill adapted to necessary
constitutional change. He preferred the oral traditions of preliterate societies where meaning can slither around, away from,
and between words in ways that become more difficult, but not
impossible, when the relationship is fixed in written documents
and defined in dictionaries.

In both preliterate and literate cultures meaning can become
more or less fixed by what McLuhan, writing with Wilfred Watson in *From Cliché to Archetype* (1970), treats as cliché, a term that
is not necessarily pejorative. It applies, to be sure, to hackneyed
literary expressions and to stock responses, both verbal and
non-verbal, of all sorts; but as with its original meaning – cliché
was the name given by printers to metal stereotypes – clichés

can be very useful. Indeed, what the literary critic Northrop
Frye defined as an archetype – 'a symbol, usually an image,
which recurs often enough in literature to be recognizable as
an element of one's literary experience as a whole' – McLuhan
terms a cliché.[52]

Clichés of this sort are treated by McLuhan in relation to what
he calls archetypes. Of these he gives many examples; but the
term itself he never defines. For our purposes here, however,
we will perhaps not stray too far from his meaning if we simplify
by letting 'archetype' denote a construct perceived as an ideal
form. (This would seem, however, to be only one of a number
of possible denotations.) Following McLuhan again, data perceived under certain circumstances as archetypal are perceived
under other circumstances as clichéd. As with figure/ground
relationships, these perceptions can reverse themselves, a relationship likened by McLuhan to the systole/diastole function of
the heart.

Using this cliché/archetype formulation, let us now examine
Innis in the context of the historiography of Canada,

VI

When Frederick Jackson Turner first treated the frontier as a
crucible and as 'the line of the most rapid and effective Americanization,' he scrapped the clichéd metaphor of European
germs developing in an American environment to contend that
the frontier experience was the archetypal American experience. Many agreed with him; so many, indeed, that the frontier
experience itself became clichéd. Thus the Canadian historian
J.M.S. Careless, writing in 1954, observed that its effects might
be observed at several different levels in the United States.
'Indeed, it may not be irrelevant to note,' he continued,

that Hollywood, that lowest common denominator of the American mind where myths are mass-produced, still pours forth a flood of highly technicoloured Westerns each purporting to touch the very soul of America, as some pioneer rugged individualist with iron hands and blazing guns 'carves out an empire' for the nation at various points west, while Indians in their thousands from Central Casting Office go down before the onward march of democracy.[53]

In perceiving the American frontier as cliché, Careless, to be sure, was dealing with the phenomenon, as he put it, 'at its lowest common denominator.' But at other more elevated levels, he discovered, 'this frontier idea is no longer as fresh and vital in its application to this country [Canada] as it was in the period before the Second World War ...'[54] What did seem to him to be 'fresh and vital' was 'Metropolitanism,' a thesis perceived as archetypal of the Canadian experience, largely contradictory of interpretations of Turner's Canadian followers, and deriving in part from Innis's *Fur Trade in Canada*. Like Innis, Careless stressed the importance of Europe and related this to communications, most notably with respect to the mid-nineteenth-century radicalism of the Toronto *Globe*. In contrast to the Turnerian explanation of the Canadian historian Frank Underhill, who had contended that the ideology of this newspaper was akin to that of Jacksonian democracy and a product of the frontier, Careless identified it with the urban, middle-class, British radicalism of Cobden and Bright, imported by its Scottish-born owner and editor, George Brown.

Thus communications theory displaced frontier theory; but it also displaced another cliché/archetype that had structured Canadian historical thought for much longer, and much more fundamentally, than the ideas of Turner. This was the cliché/archetype of 'responsible government.'

This expression, which had been the political slogan of the Baldwinite reform party in the 1830s and 1840s, would shift its content in several ways in an interesting and very significant fashion. Understood literally, the term came to mean cabinet responsibility to elected representatives in a parliamentary form of government; but in the late nineteenth and early twentieth centuries three variant implications were attached to this meaning. Two of these were contradictory of each other; the third masked the contradiction. To one school of *imperially oriented* historians, the achievement of responsible government in Canada implied that a separatist, republican impulse, born of an imperfect form of colonial government, had been overcome, and that, in consequence of this achievement, the political and cultural ties with the mother country, Great Britain, would remain unsevered. To another group of *nationally oriented* writers, however, the achievement of responsible government came to imply that Canada would become an autonomous, independent nation with a distinctive culture of its own. To a third parcel of historians, who celebrated the British Commonwealth of Nations as an advanced and superior form of empire, it confusingly implied both.

To begin to understand the cliché/archetype function of the expression, one must observe how it has shifted its meaning and observe also the confusion of thought that has attended the shift. As suggested above, the term today means cabinet responsibility to a popularly elected chamber in a parliamentary form of democracy with *complete* executive authority vested in the cabinet. But in 1839, following the unsuccessful rebellions of 1837–8, the governor and high commissioner, Lord Durham, published a report in which he recommended not this but a very restricted form of local ministerial responsibility with important powers reserved to the imperial authorities in England. He occasionally used the phrase 'responsible government,' but it meant no more than the opposite of arbitrary government. Thus he referred to citizens of the United States as living under 'a perfectly free and eminently responsible government.'*

---

* I have treated this and much else that follows in 'An Enduring Canadian

By reason of politics related to the form of government given to the Canadas in 1841, however, the term soon acquired the more restricted meaning of cabinet responsibility to the elected members. But there was no agreement among politicians then, nor among historians long after, as to whether the term 'responsible government' referred to the structure of government conceded in 1841 or whether it applied only to the form Baldwinite reformers struggled for, which was conceded after 1848. The difference was that in 1841 the governor, and through him the Colonial Office in Britain, retained a measure of independence and executive control, whereas after 1848 this power passed to the local cabinet.

At issue here were questions of cultural identity about which Canadians had been long divided, and had long felt strongly; for the autonomist implications of the concession of 1848 were a long time working themselves out. Indeed they were only finally settled with the passage of the Statute of Westminster in 1931, one year after Innis published *The Fur Trade in Canada*.

Meanwhile, it was one thing for many English Canadians to assail local 'wicked advisers of the crown' – termed 'the Family Compact' – in the name of responsible government; it was quite another to seek to dismember the British Empire. It was within this context that Canadian historians argued about the term, its historical significance, and what it implied for the future. Specious, often irrelevant, discussions of its origins and meaning masked deep divisions of opinion.

Some of these very linearly minded writers contended that the acquisition of responsible government strengthened ties with the mother country; others that it heralded the advent of a new and independent nation. Of the latter school, the most influential historian was John Charles Dent who in 1881 published *The Last Forty Years: The Union of 1841 to Confederation*.

Myth: Responsible Government and the Family Compact,' *Journal of Canadian Studies* 12 (1977).

Dent was obsessed by his archetypal concept of responsible government.* As his recent editor, Donald Swainson, has remarked: 'His linear development ran not from the "struggle" for responsible government to the present, but from the famous "struggle" to a future condition. His preferred future involved Canada independent of Great Britain.'[55] Dent was a historian with a mission. As Swainson further remarks, his use of history 'was similar to twentieth century historians who stress "relevancy" and tend to utilize selected aspects of the past as part of their personal battle to shape the future.'

Scarcely less archetypal, however, was the concept of responsible government entertained by historians quite opposed to the objectives of Dent. One such writer was Stephen Leacock, best remembered as the humorist who satirized the parochialism of the imaginary community of Mariposa in *Sunshine Sketches of a Little Town* (1912). This satire, as figure, had the same ground as his theories about empire and government. Leacock, like Innis a political economist, was a man who declared himself to be an imperialist because he declined to be provincial.† And when he published *Baldwin, Lafontaine, Hincks: Responsible Government* in 1907, Leacock, humorist though he was, did not find responsible government – the 'corner-stone of the British Empire' as he argued – a concept at which to poke fun.

With the publication of *The Fur Trade in Canada* in 1930, however, figure/ground relations shifted; and responsible government became an object of scornful mirth. Observe Donald Creighton dealing with the story of the famous struggle: 'This interpretation has ... its solemn side, its aspect heroic and almost sacred, with prophets such as Baldwin, wise kings such as Lord

* For more on Dent see G.H. Patterson, 'Dent, John Charles,' *Dictionary of Canadian Biography*, vol. 11 (Toronto, Buffalo, London 1982), 246–9.

† For Leacock and the imperialism he exemplified see Carl Berger, *The Sense of Power: Studies in the Ideas of Canadian Imperialism, 1867–1914* (Toronto 1970).

Elgin, great moments of deliverance from bondage as with the formation of the Reform Ministry in 1848, and terrible plagues and tribulations as when Metcalfe and Head were sent to smite the chosen people.'[56] And he pointed to the stereotyped biography that was allied with this clichéd mythology.

Is it possible that, even in Canada, people can actually be so indistinguishably alike? Is there really only one Canadian statesman, whose metamorphoses have merely involved a change of name? Or are all Canadian statesmen simply members of the same family, a spiritual family at any rate, with certain persistent and unchangeable family characteristics and a distinguished hyphenated surname? Are there really biographies of Baldwin, Hincks, and Laurier, or are these merely lives of Robert Responsible-Government, Francis Responsible-Government, and Wilfrid Responsible-Government?[57]

An interpretation of history could scarcely be viewed as being more clichéd.

It is significant, however, that while Creighton held the hagiography of this school in contempt, and while he viewed the interpretation he ridiculed as simplistic, and while he despised the objectives of writers like Dent, he did not conceive of 'the struggle for responsible government' and its consequences as pure fiction. For the general outlines of the story – the cliché, if you will – informs his own *Dominion of the North*, which was published in 1944. But, on the other hand, he was certainly excited by the archetypal possibilities suggested by Innis's communications theory, not least because its implications seemed to be contradictory of the achievement of responsible government as interpreted by a Dent.

Creighton identified the archetype/cliché he assailed not with imperially minded but passé writers like Leacock, but with their autonomist opponents who wrote in what he took to be a continentalist 'Liberal' tradition. That is why he coupled biographies of Prime Minister Wilfrid Laurier, who had only just been born in 1841, with those of others who had actually struggled for the achievement of 1848. Creighton, applying ideas derived from Innis, was trying to supersede this tradition. For this reason, he ignored, did not think of, or dismissed as irrelevant, the common *ground* that lay behind the *figure* of the interpretation of the achievement of responsible government given by writers like Leacock, and the *figure* of his own Laurentian thesis. This common ground was common opposition to ideas of separation from Britain and isolation from Europe.

These ideas of separation and isolation were very old in North America. They had once informed the 'Farewell Address' of George Washington, the minds of revolutionaries in the War of Independence, the thought of the Puritan founders of New England, and much else in the American experience. After 1893 they are to be found embedded in the frontier thesis of Frederick Jackson Turner. But these same ideas are by no means alien to the Canadian experience. They are to be discovered, in modified form, for example, in the writings of John Charles Dent;* and, before his time they are to be discovered in the polemic of republican opponents of the several administrations of pre-Confederation British North America.

In contrast to this school of thought, Creighton, through Innis, had discovered a new way of declining to be provincial. From a diachronic perspective, Creighton merely superseded this group and that of Leacock. But, from a synchronic point of view, both he and Leacock wrote within the same polemical tradition. Older than the American War of Independence, this was the eighteenth-century American Tory tradition of those United Empire Loyalists who argued and pamphleteered against the American Whigs. Within the United States, rhetorical conflict of this sort ended in 1783 with the Peace of Versailles.

* See my article on Dent in *Dictionary of Canadian Biography*, vol II.

But within the remaining North American colonies of George III it raged on for a great many years to come.* The enduring nature of this counter-revolutionary, Tory tradition, of which Creighton and Leacock are exemplary, may in large measure be attributed to the communications system of the St Lawrence that bound Canada to Europe in the fashion indicated by Innis.

VII

What then of the communications theory of Innis in Canadian history today? As is suggested by the work and thought of the severest critic of *The Fur Trade in Canada*, much of it is embedded as cliché/archetype in the writings of contemporary historians. It has thereby escaped the mechanized, fossilizing form of Innis's own printed books. Had these ideas not become clichéd, they would now be forgotten. But most of Innis's later ideas, and what McLuhan made of them, have had almost no influence on the historiographical ground to which they are related as figure. We shall return to these ideas in the following chapters.

---

* For the eighteenth-century beginnings of this debate see W.H. Nelson, *The American Tory* (Oxford 1961).

THREE

CONCEPTS
MODELS
AND
METAPHORS

I

In his last years Harold Innis was preoccupied with concepts of time and space as they related to the study of history. The concepts he himself entertained, however, and precisely what he thought about time and space, are sometimes less than clear. 'History – product of west in terms of linear progress of time,' he noted in his 'Idea File,' 'Contrast with China. Use of centuries – fingers and toes – distortion of history.'[1]* Also somewhat bewildering is the title given to his last book, *Changing Concepts of Time*.

The title is curious in that, at first sight, the book's five chapters – 'The Strategy of Culture,' 'Military Implications of the American Empire,' 'Roman Law and the British Empire,' 'The Press, a Neglected Factor in the Economic History of the Twentieth Century,' and 'Great Britain, the United States and Canada' – seem to have little or nothing to do with concepts of time. Apart from some references to *Time* magazine and to *The Times* of London, the book's index contains only two references to time. 'Law,' Innis observed on page 58 with respect to the common law, 'is apt to become anything boldly asserted and plausibly maintained. A neglect of the time problem implies a lack of interest in theoretical problems. In contrast, the Roman law tradition in its concern with principles attracts the highest intellectual ability to the academic field and encourages an interest in philosophical theory and theoretical speculation.' And on page 108 he noted in passing: 'The Chinese concept of time ... as plural and characterized by a succession of times, which reflects their social organization with its interest in hierarchy

---

* My interpretation of this entry is: In contrast with the manner in which history was understood in ancient China, the linear idea of progress is peculiar to the west. The division of time into centuries, which are divisible by ten, the number of a man's fingers and toes, which gave rise to the decimal system, has distorted man's understanding of history.

and relative stability, as well as their concept of space, has been adapted through collective collaboration and experience to social life. The Western concept of time with its linear character, reinforced by the use of the decimal system, has in contrast a capacity for infinite extension to the past and the future and a limited capacity for adaptation.' But these two remarks are so buried in the text of the book that they would most probably escape the attention of any reader not intent upon searching them out.

What the title signified to Innis is more directly indicated by an acknowledgment he made to the classicist E.A. Havelock. Eric Havelock had taught for seventeen years at Victoria College in the University of Toronto before moving in 1947 to Harvard and from thence to Yale. Innis was much indebted to him.

It was believed by Marshall McLuhan that Havelock had picked up the idea of examining the effects of the introduction of the technology of writing into ancient Greece from Innis. Certainly Havelock brilliantly explored this idea in *Preface to Plato*, which was published in 1963, eleven years after the death of Innis. McLuhan's supposition, therefore, was not entirely unreasonable. Recently, however, Havelock denied the connection to suggest that he and Innis had each hit upon the idea independently.[2]

Innis's private correspondence reveals that he was much more familiar with Havelock's thesis than the latter later recalled. 'I have just read a book,' he wrote in 1951,

by [I.A.] Richards called *Mencius on the Mind* raising the question of understanding Chinese culture. E.A. Havelock in a recent book *The Crucifixion of Intellectual Man*, now at Harvard and formerly a student of F.M. Cornford, has been concerned with the same problem in Greece. He thinks that the mention [*sic*] of Greek culture as far as the Greeks were concerned began to change between 410 and 405 B.C. when they started to educate the youth systematically. *He has a manu-*

script on the question of the shift from the oral to the written tradition in Greek
culture which he hopes to complete this summer. (emphasis mine)[3]

Thus it is most probable, although not absolutely certain, that it was Innis whose attention was first directed to 'the shift from the oral to the written tradition' by Havelock; and not the other way around.

Be this as it may, Havelock is very helpful in assessing the influence of classical scholarship on Innis. Himself a Cambridge graduate, he thought Innis was fortunate to have had a Canadian background and little formal training in the classics. 'His intellectual roots,' Havelock observed,

grew in the Canadian soil out of a Canadian experience. They of course owed a debt to European nourishment, but in this connection, speaking myself as a classicist, I would venture to call attention to a certain educational advantage he may have enjoyed, in avoiding Oxford, which several of his academic contemporaries had attended as Rhodes Scholars, in favour of Chicago. At Oxford sixty years ago, had he taken 'Greats' (the present degree in Philosophy, Politics and Economics only came into existence about that time) he would have been exposed to an intensely urbanized and urbane community, highly literate and conscious of the fact, and to an intellectual climate still pervaded by the philosophical assumptions of neo-idealism, as these had taken hold in the writings and teachings of Green, Bradley and Bosanquet. Had he been introduced to classic Greece, he would have been required to view it in terms of the achievement of ideals, moral, political and spiritual, certainly not in terms of technology, still less the technology of communication.[4]

In contrast to some of Innis's colleagues in economics and history, Havelock thought well of his entry into the fields of classics and communications. Certainly he thought he was attending to

the right authorities. 'It is ... significant ... to observe,' Havelock
wrote,

that, as his own footnotes reveal, he was absorbing at this time the
seminal writings of four classical scholars: F.M. Cornford, whose Cambridge lectures on the Presocratics had ... first taught me that the task
of the historian of early Greek thought is, in William James' terms, to
understand 'foreign states of mind'; Milman Parry, the founding father
of the oral theory of Homeric composition; Rhys Carpenter, who had
recently established the comparatively late and correct date for the
introduction of the Greek alphabet; and Martin Nilsson, whose *Homer
and Mycenae* may be said to have put together the overall picture of the
early Greek consciousness.[5]

Of these scholars, all of them students of the *mind* of ancient
Greece, special note should be taken of F.M. Cornford – Havelock's teacher who sought to understand foreign states of mind
by the light of the psychology of William James – to whom we
must return below.

Before that, however, we must turn again to the preface
of *Changing Concepts of Time*. Innis there asserted that he had
attempted to elaborate the thesis contained in *The Bias of Communication* and *Empire and Communications*. Just what this thesis was,
he neglected to specify; but it will be recalled that both these
works were informed by concepts of space and time that were
peculiarly his own. Just as in writing *Empire and Communications*
he had assumed the reader's background knowledge of his
earlier *Fur Trade in Canada*, so too he here assumed familiarity
with other of his work.

Innis remarked in the preface that he had here assumed 'that
different civilizations regard the concepts of space and time in
different ways and that even the same civilization ... differs
widely in attitude at different periods and in different areas.'
Political boundaries and the character of political institutions,

he added, will reflect these varying concepts in themselves. In explaining these differences 'emphasis has been given,' he asserted, 'to technological changes in communications.' His general argument, he then surprisingly observed, 'has been powerfully developed in the *Prometheus Bound* of Aeschylus as outlined by E.A. Havelock in *The Crucifixion of Intellectual Man* (Boston, 1951).'[6]

In *The Crucifixion of Intellectual Man* Havelock had published his new translation of *Prometheus Bound* along with an extended introduction such as Aeschylus himself perhaps might have written had he been George Bernard Shaw addressing the twentieth century in a lengthy preface. At any rate, it was this introduction that caught the attention of Innis.

The hero of the play, Havelock commented, was the rebel god Prometheus – the 'forethinker,' as his name signified – who presented the stolen technology of fire to man and who in consequence, by the command of Zeus, was now bound in fetters and tormented.

The gaze of the dramatist, as it retraces the old story, has concentrated upon its conclusion, the visitation of a jealous punishment, which he presents as a crucifixion and a Passion. But the depth and poignancy of historical meaning which he puts into this interpretation depend upon certain improvements which he has made in the old myth, and these are fundamental. Fire is no longer the instrument of the savage, used for cooking and warmth. It has become the 'technological flame,' and its primary uses and applications are virtually ignored. It is treated as the excuse for the introduction of a whole array of those tools and skills which build the structure of a civilized life.[7]

Thus, according to Havelock, the stolen fire symbolized 'energy'; and Aeschylus was treating a situation attendant upon technological innovation.

According to Havelock, this powerful drama had much to say

to an age in which technological innovation on a grand scale had led to massive destruction at Hiroshima. The nuclear physicists of the last half century, he observed, 'were just professors pursuing in relative obscurity a mathematical dream, in service to the purest, the most abstract type of science and, it seemed, the most useless.' Did any of them in Cambridge or Copenhagen or Berlin or Moscow or Paris or New York, he inquired, 'foresee Hiroshima, and the hysteria of nations, and the naked power-politics of the Bomb?'[8]

With what appears to have been a Jungian approach to myth in mind, Havelock observed that the bitter dialectic of *Prometheus* seemed to pursue us still. The old myth upon which Aeschylus had founded his tragedy was 'one of those universal myths, in which even the savage seems able to express accurate premonition of what his descendants will one day encounter. It is as though the collective consciousness of the human species were a continuous thing, living outside the confines of time, able to guess the dark meaning of its history before that history has been realized.'[9] But twentieth-century man, who lacked 'forethought,' seemed quite unable to profit from this understanding.

It is here that Havelock's thought most closely touched that of Innis. The problem, according to Havelock, was that, by reason of modern physics, a revolution was taking place in our concepts of space and time.

Our relationship to time and space is no more a matter of metaphysics but of precise calculation, and the calculation yields an equation which crushes us by its reduction of our stature ... The knowledge is too much for us, and it may yet kill us ... To know these things, and to live with this knowledge, is the special burden of our age. Intellectual man of the nineteenth century was the first to estimate with precision his total lowliness, his absolute nullity, in space and time. That is the secret shock administered to our culture.[10]

Man had been unable to come to terms with his new knowledge.

This seems to have been what Innis declared to be the general argument with which he agreed. But to observe its relationship to his thought we must return to *The Bias of Communication* and *Empire and Communications*, the two works in which, he declared, his underlying thesis had been worked out.

II

In previous chapters we have had occasion to emphasize the unity of the early and late work of Innis. In his last years, however, he dealt with the shift from the nineteenth-century Newtonian model of actuality to new post-Einstein models; and this was quite different from anything he had previously concerned himself with.

In contrast to Einstein, observes Dudley Shapere, Newton believed that the laws of motion presupposed the existence of an absolute space and time in which bodies could truly, rather than relatively, be said to be in motion.

A body that appears to be in accelerated motion relative to some material reference frame would only appear to be in the presence of forces relative to that frame and would appear to be free of forces relative to some other reference frame. Although Newton admitted that, in general, measurements of velocity must be made relative to a material reference frame, he claimed that the presence of absolute motion could be distinguished from relative motion in certain cases by its 'properties, causes and effects.'[11]

Einstein rejected these absolute Newtonian concepts to assert the principle of relativity as a fundamental general law of physics. His theory, writes G.J. Whitrow,

implies that observers in uniform motion relative to one another will, in general, assign different times to the same event and that a moving clock will appear to run slow compared with an identical clock at relative rest. Also, a body in relative motion will be regarded as having a shorter length in the direction of its motion than it has for an observer for whom it is at relative rest ... [These effects] imply that all statements concerning space and time have a meaning only when referred to a definite observer.[12]

Beyond this, Einstein treated time as a 'fourth dimension,' as part of the 'time/space continuum.'

In the eighteenth and nineteenth centuries Newton's theories had a well-known revolutionary impact on both scientific and non-scientific fields of inquiry. 'Nature and Nature's laws lay hid in night; / God said "Let Newton be!" and all was light,' wrote Alexander Pope. Newton's mechanical theory gave rise to the governing metaphor of the clockwork universe, to Deism and to history and economic theory founded upon concepts of 'natural law.'

It is the impact of Newton's theories upon history and economic theory that concerns us here. Innis, despite his admiration for Adam Smith, reacted strongly against 'mechanical' interpretations of both history and economics. The Smith whom he admired was the economist who had attacked archaic monopolies and tariff barriers that hindered the free flow of trade, even as rigid written constitutions obstruct necessary political change and outmoded concepts impede the flow of new ideas. 'My bias,' he declared, 'is with the oral tradition, particularly as reflected in Greek civilization, and with the necessity of recapturing something of its spirit. For that purpose we should try to understand something of the importance of life or of the living tradition, which is peculiar to the oral as against the mechanized tradition, and of the contributions of Greek civilization.'[13]

The expression 'mechanized tradition,' as Innis here used it, referred specifically to Marxist interpretations of history and economics; but it also referred more generally to the mechanical tradition within which Marx wrote, which was that of Isaac Newton and René Descartes. The 'living tradition' he set in opposition to it was that of ancient Greece – which he, Cornford, and Havelock sought to unite with that of Werner Heisenberg, Niels Bohr, Albert Einstein, and the rest.

It is with the latter group of thinkers that the late work has much in common. The media of communication are treated by Innis as *relative* to each other. Relative to clay tablets, parchment was possessed of a bias of space; relative to contemporary newsprint it was biased with respect to time. They are not treated as absolute categories. And to think about media in this fashion would seem to imply some sort of time-space continuum rather than two discrete categories.

III

Harold Innis did not have a tidy mind. Because he tended to think dialectically and non-sequentially, his work is full of contradictions that are not always easy to understand. It is clear, however, that he never just accepted modern physics as presented to him by expert authorities. He sometimes disagreed with them. At the risk of imposing a misleading order upon his random thought, let us examine some of these differences.

In certain enigmatic essays, published in *The Bias of Communication*, Innis treated time and space, tracing their effects from antiquity to modern times. Our problem here is not simply to review or assess that material; it is to discover the concepts of space and time entertained by Innis himself. For these he never *directly* asserted.

Behind the opaque introductory paragraph of the essay 'The Problem of Space' are to be discerned some ideas derived from the relativity theory of Albert Einstein and others derived from elsewhere. ' "Space and time," ' wrote Innis, ' "and also their space-time product, fall into their places as mere mental frameworks of our own constitution [*sic*]." Gauss held that whereas number was a product of the mind, space had a reality outside the mind whose laws cannot be described *a priori*. In the history of thought, especially of mathematics, Cassirer remarked, "at times, the concept of space, at other times, the concept of numbers, took the lead." '[14] The three sentences in this paragraph are not serially and logically related; they are simply juxtaposed. How they relate to the rest of the essay is not immediately evident; for in the next paragraph Innis turns to a consideration of problems of space and time in the ancient civilizations of Egypt and Mesopotamia without a paragraph, or even a sentence, of transition. To discover the meaning of this introductory paragraph, one must first recover the context within which he wrote.

The first sentence – ' "Space and time, and also their space-time product, fall into their places as mere mental frameworks of our own constitution" ' – is a quotation from a source Innis identified only as 'President of the British Association, 1934,' who proves upon investigation to have been the physicist Sir Arthur Eddington. Eddington was being quoted by Havelock's old teacher, the Cambridge classicist Francis Cornford, in an article entitled 'The Invention of Space.'

'Neither space nor time is found to exist in its own right,' Eddington had remarked,

but only as a way of cutting up something more comprehensive – the space-time continuum. Thus we find that space and time cannot be classified as realities of nature, and the generalized theory of relativity shows that the same is true of their product, the space-time continuum. This can be crumpled and twisted and warped as much as we please without becoming one whit less true to nature – which, of course, can only mean that it is not itself part of nature. Space and time, and also their space-time product, fall into their places as mere mental frameworks of our own construction.[15]

What we took for the steel structure of the universe, Cornford concluded from this, turns out to be less like steel than india-rubber, which itself exists only as an arbitrary figment of the human brain. 'How, ' he inquired, 'did the illusion of the steel framework, as an external fact, come to be imposed upon common sense?'

Euclidean geometry, Cornford continued, is based upon the assumption that space is infinite. But modern physics had established that this could not be the case. If the infinite extension of three-dimensional space is no more than the construction of the human brain, when and by whom was it constructed? The post-Euclidean finite but unbounded space, Cornford concluded, 'takes us back to the pre-Euclidean finite but boundless sphere of Anaximander, Parmenides, and Empedocles. These philosophers did not know as much mathematics as Einstein; but they had the advantage over Newton in knowing much less mathematics than Euclid. They had not been misled by geometry into projecting its infinite space into the external world under the name of the Void.'[16] The Euclidean era itself, that is to say from about 300 BC right up to the twentieth century, Cornford was further to conclude, 'presents itself as a period of aberration, in which common sense was reluctantly lured away from the position that it has now, with no less reluctance, to regain.'

The second sentence in Innis's introductory paragraph – 'Gauss held that whereas number was a product of the mind, space had a reality outside the mind whose laws can not be described *a priori*' – is set in apposition to the one we have just examined. It relates to another problem in epistemology: that posed by the nineteenth-century development of a new, apparently self-contradictory non-Euclidean geometry. This had been treated by Ernst Cassirer in *The Problem of Knowledge: Philosophy, Science and History since Hegel*, a book from which Innis worked and to which we must turn here.

Leibniz, observed Cassirer, would not allow the axioms of Euclid to stand as absolutely undemonstrable propositions, and the demand for their proof ran through all his philosophical and mathematical writings. Even for such propositions as that the whole is greater than its parts, Leibniz offered an explicit proof. 'Thus,' wrote Cassirer, 'the belief in the immediate certainty and persuasiveness of geometrical "evidence" was profoundly shaken within the confines of classical rationalism itself, not to be reinstated even by Kant's a priori forms of pure intuition – if this theory be interpreted in its true sense, "transcendentally," instead of psychologically.'[17] Hume had initially extended his doubting even to mathematical knowledge to declare it invalid as measured by his standard of truth, sensory perception. But he later retracted this judgment to concede certainty to mathematics in view of the argument that it refers not to *matters of fact* but solely to *relations of ideas*. Between mathematical ideas there are necessary and unalterable relations that depend upon nothing that exists in the universe but purely upon the activity of thought.

Rationalists and empiricists, Cassirer observed, seemed fully in agreement about this until the beginning of the nineteenth century.

Then suddenly they were shaken in their belief as the first systems of non-Euclidean geometry appeared. If geometry owes its certainty to pure reason, how strange that this reason can arrive at entirely different and wholly incongruous systems, while claiming equal truth for each. Does this not call in question the infallibility of reason itself? Does not reason in its very essence become contradictory and ambiguous? To recognize a plurality of geometries seemed to mean renouncing the unity of reason, which is its intrinsic and distinguishing feature.[18]

Karl Friedrich Gauss, to whom Innis referred, had been the first mathematician to become aware of these problems.

In all the history of mathematics, wrote Cassirer,

there are few events of such immediate and decisive importance for the shaping and development of the problem of knowledge as the discovery of the various forms of non-Euclidean geometry. Gauss, the pioneer, who seems to have been in possession of all its fundamental concepts as early as the beginning of the nineteenth century, hardly dared mention them at first. He guarded his secret carefully because he had no hope that the new problem would be understood and because, as he said in a letter, he feared the 'hue and cry of the blockheads.'[19]

The blockheads were those unable or unwilling to abandon the traditional but now outmoded concept of space.

Rationalism, Cassirer observed, remained firmly convinced that mathematics is the paragon of *a priori* knowledge. Kant had declared mathematics to be a shining example of progress that could be made in knowledge independently of experience.

But the value and cogency of his illustration appeared to be seriously undermined by the discovery of non-Euclidean geometry. Here Gauss immediately drew the most radical consequences for the theory of knowledge. Arithmetic and analysis, based as they are on the idea of pure number, remained for him the purely rational knowledge. *He dismissed geometry, however, from their company, and placed it on the side of the empirical sciences.* Thus he was led to attempt a solution of the problem 'which geometry is true,' which is the one existing in reality, by measurements on empirical bodies. 'We must humbly confess,' he wrote in a letter to Bessel, 'that whereas number is a product of the mind space has a reality outside the mind whose laws we cannot *prescribe* a priori.' (emphasis mine)[20]

Taking note that Innis has transcribed the word 'prescribe' as 'describe,' we are now in a position to relate this second sentence – 'Gauss held that whereas number was a product of the mind, space had a reality outside the mind whose laws cannot be described [*sic*] *a priori*' – to the first sentence – ' "Space and time, and also their space-time product, fall into their places as mere mental frameworks of our own constitution." ' It means that Innis was playing off Gauss against Einstein, that he was toying with the idea that, while time may have no reality outside the mind, the same thing cannot be said of space.

The third sentence – 'In the history of thought, especially of mathematics, Cassirer remarked, "at times the concept of space, at other times the concept of numbers, took the lead" ' – can be dealt with more expeditiously. Cassirer was referring to a conflict among physicists over mechanics and energetics. The dispute itself need not detain us here, our concern being with a comment Cassirer made upon it. 'In order to understand this opposition,' he wrote,

it is necessary to go back to its roots in the theory of knowledge. The conflict was essentially between two different motives, each one indispensable in the construction of the edifice of scientific knowledge. The exclusion of either was not to be thought of, though there was room for argument as to which should be accorded the central position and real supremacy. *At times, the concept of space, at other times the concept of number, took the lead* ... (emphasis mine)[21]

Innis does not appear to have concerned himself elsewhere in the essay with the concept of number; but what Cassirer had to say about the historical relationship of the concept of space with that of number resembles Innis's contention that at times in the history of civilizations concepts of space were dominant and at other times concepts of time. Cassirer pointed to a *dialectical* relationship between the concepts of space and number that corresponds to a way in which Innis looked at space and time.

One of the clearest statements Innis ever made with respect to the concepts of modern physics appears in a review he wrote of Sir James Jeans's *Physics and Philosophy* (Cambridge 1943). Innis praised the clarity of Jeans's writing, but took significant issue with his categories. The title of the volume, the headings of chapters, and the arrangement of its contents suggested a fundamental weakness. 'Philosophy is concerned with the whole range of knowledge including physics and cannot be regarded as separate from physics or as subordinate to it as the title implies. The changing place of physics in philosophy would have been a title implying a proper and more respectful relationship.'[22] Innis was not just resurrecting an old concept of 'natural philosophy'; he was opposing, as he often did, the specialization and fragmentation of learning.

Jeans, according to Innis, had increased the debt of gratitude owed to him by lay readers for his clearness in stating problems of significance to modern thought. Prior to acknowledging this debt, Innis had specifically indicated the 'problems of significance to modern thought' elucidated by him.

Science, the author states, has added two new worlds – 'the world of man lies just about half-way between the world of the electron and the world of the nebulae. Elaborate studies made with instrumental aid have shown that the phenomena of the world of the electron do not in any way form a replica on a minute scale of the phenomena of the man-sized world, and neither are these latter a replica on a minute scale of the phenomena of the world of the nebulae.' (42–3) In the man-sized world, Kant elaborated forms such as space and time, of perception and understanding in the structure of the mind which perceives the world, while Alexander made mind the creation of space and time returning to 'the Aristotelian conception of categories as forms of the world itself.' (69) 'Causality and the possibility of representation in space and time – prevail in the man-sized world but not in the small-scale world of atomic physics. They would seem to be ingrained rather than inborn, not so much laws that we thrust on nature as laws that we – with our limited knowledge of the world – have allowed nature to thrust on us.' (71)

The contributions of physicists concluding in 1917 with Einstein's linking up of the laws of radioactive transformation with the laws of Planck's quantum theory brought about the complete abdication of determinism 'not only from the domain of radioactivity, but from the whole realm of physics.' (151) 'The classical physics seemed to bolt and bar the door leading to any sort of freedom of the will; the new physics hardly does this: it almost seems to suggest that the door may be unlocked – if only we could find the handle. Determinism and freedom, matter and naturalism need to be redefined in the light of our new scientific knowledge. Modern physics has moved in the direction of mentalism.' (216)

Innis was impressed by all this.

But the root of error, he added, followed Jeans's 'approach as a physicist.'

It may be that the concepts of space and time break down in the approach to other worlds [Jeans had distinguished between the man-sized world, the world of the electron, and the world of the nebulae] and that new concepts become essential, but it is significant that the worlds other than the man-sized world concern a very small number for a very small amount of time. There remain the problems on which physics and science generally have comparatively little to contribute – namely the problems of human society. In largely evading these they evade the problems of philosophy. The neglect of these problems and the naivete of separating physics and philosophy as two voices constitute the chief danger of the efforts to popularize science. Energy is drained from the most difficult problems of civilization into a general glorification of the advances of science.

Innis then concluded by setting in abrupt apposition to the foregoing an assertion of the importance of studying myth. 'Professor Toynbee in *A Study of History*,' he wrote, 'has shown the significance of the myth as a tool for the unlocking of mysteries of civilization. We cannot disregard his achievements lightly in spite of the contributions of science.'

In previous chapters we have examined Innis's early communications theory with respect to river systems and the distinction he made between the systems themselves and their shifting content. We have noted the interest he had in studying the effects such communications systems had in shaping communities dependent upon them; and the even greater interest he took in what happened when one communications system was superseded by another. Innis long continued to study structural problems in this fashion, all of which owed nothing to modern physics. Beginning with the late work, however, he began to write about the *relativity*, or 'bias,' of media both in relation to each other and in relation to space and time. In this instance his pattern of thought resembles relativity theory, which he probably took as a model to escape the 'mechanical' theory he so disliked and mistrusted. It offered him an escape from determinism.

IV

In previous chapters we have taken note of significant differences in the thought of Innis and that of his interpreter Donald Creighton. The latter was certainly influenced by the thesis of *The Fur Trade in Canada*. And despite the fact that that thesis as later developed by Innis influenced him scarcely at all, Innis remained most favourably impressed by his friend's work. Shortly before his death he read the proofs of the first volume of Creighton's biography of Sir John A. Macdonald. 'You are to be congratulated on its publication,' he wrote to the book's publisher. 'It marks definitely a new development in the style of writing Canadian history and it will compel a rewriting of much of Canadian history which has been slanted toward the liberal view and had left almost neglected its most important figure in the history of Confederation. It is difficult to speak too highly of the volume.'[23] Two months earlier he had written to Creighton that he believed his book would be 'the most significant origin [sic] of our generation and nothing must be allowed to interfere with it.'[24]

Despite such comments, the views of Innis and those of Creighton, whether they themselves fully realized it or not, and they seem not to have, were in significant ways quite opposed. As noted previously, this is most apparent with respect to their conflicting notions about the nature of the Canadian federal system and the statute upon which it was founded. Creighton was an extreme centralist; Innis was a hardly less extreme decentralist. Scarcely less opposed were their differing concepts of space and time. As we have also noted, Creighton had a linearly biased understanding of his friend's late work.

This linear bias is reflected by the metaphors Creighton chose for the titles of two of his books. One was *The Road to Confederation*; the other was *The Forked Road*. In the first he viewed Canadian history as moving in the right direction; in the latter he argued to the contrary. Both metaphors imply that history has direction and were far from resembling the metaphors and models derived from modern physics or ancient China and Greece that engaged the attention of Innis. Creighton's concepts of time and space were conventional, linear, assumed, and fixed.

The way in which Creighton initially responded to Innis's early work is clearly revealed in an essay, 'The Commercial Class in Canadian Politics, 1792–1840,' published in 1933. The British conquest of Canada, he argued, had infused into the province of Quebec a peculiarly American spirit, which was embodied in the American traders who followed in the wake of the conquering British army. And this American spirit, he contended, 'was fundamentally materialistic. It was the response of a middle-class population in a commercially minded age to the apparently unbounded possibilities of an unworked continent ... It was this energy and commercial aggressiveness which the "miserable sutlers and traders" brought to Quebec and Montreal. They came ... with the single, simple, American objective of making money by trade.'[25] They had recognized the possibilities of the St Lawrence–Great Lakes waterways.

In Quebec these materialists came into contact with the very different culture of the conquered French, one that, according to Creighton, was essentially anachronistic. Cut off by conquest from its French metropolis, French Canada had been 'decapitated.'* The conquest, he wrote, 'brought not merely an administrative but also a commercial decapitation. And this gradual but inevitable concentration of commercial leadership in the hands of British traders accentuated the basically peasant and professional character of French-Canadian society.'[26]

This antithesis, conceived of as existing between English- and French-Canadian societies, had been even more sharply delineated the previous year in 'The Struggle for Financial Control in Lower Canada, 1818–1831.' There Creighton treated the struggle for the power of the purse fought out between the French-dominated House of Assembly and the several gover-

---

* The 'decapitation hypothesis' is usually believed to have originated not with Creighton but with historians at the Université de Montréal.

nors of the colony. Parallel struggles had occurred in other British colonies, he conceded, but here it 'has this additional and special significance.'

> ... it was not a quarrel between two ambitious groups who cherished the same dreams of prosperity and who accepted the same economic gospel. It was a contest between two classes, between two ages of economic and social development, between the France which the political revolution had destroyed, and the England which the industrial revolution had created. A peasant and professional community, unambitious, parsimonious, and unmoved by the lush economic possibilities of a new land, was confronted by a governing class whose deepest instincts were towards improvement, expansion, and prosperity.[27]

This was to marry a new set of ideas borrowed from Innis to an old cliché/archetype, that is, to an eighteenth- and nineteenth-century concept of 'progress.'

When Creighton began to write history that concept was only just beginning to be questioned by historians. Oswald Spengler's *Decline of the West* had appeared in 1918; but in its view history still had direction. J.B. Bury's *The Idea of Progress: An Inquiry into Its Origin and Growth* was published in 1928. 'Enough has been said,' wrote Bury, 'to show that the Progress of humanity belongs to the same order of ideas as Providence or personal immortality. It is true or it is false, and like them it cannot be proved either true or false. Belief in it is an act of faith.'[28] Herbert Butterfield's *The Whig Interpretation of History* was first published in 1931, the year in which the Creighton article quoted from above also appeared. Butterfield treated an interpretation of history that was informed by a linear metaphor of time and was by no means confined to 'Whigs.' This study, wrote he,

> deals with 'the whig interpretation of history' in what I conceive to be the accepted meaning of the phrase ... What is discussed is the tendency

in many historians to write on the side of Protestants and Whigs, to praise revolutions provided they have been successful, to emphasise certain principles of progress in the past and to produce a story which is the ratification if not the glorification of the present. This whig version of the course of history is associated with certain methods of historical organisation and inference – certain fallacies to which all history is liable, unless it be historical research ...[29]

Butterfield was dealing with a historical interpretation he held to be specious; Creighton was dealing with 'the ratification if not the glorification' of a political and economic program of late-eighteenth-century and nineteenth-century Montreal merchants that he conceived of as underpinning contemporary Canada. He shared many of those merchants' ideas, including a concept of time.

From a historiographical point of view, Creighton recognized some of his own limitations. In an address to students at York University entitled 'History and Literature,' he concluded by remarking that he did not consider his talk to be a solid contribution to the theory or philosophy of history, or even a detailed plan for writing it. 'When I began to write,' he confessed, 'I had no plan at all, and not much knowledge of what the philosophers of history had said. I designed and wrote my books instinctively and not in conscious accordance with any literary principles.'[30] But Creighton did structure the raw data of history; and the way he did so reveals something of the structure of his own mind.

In this respect his comments on eighteenth- and nineteenth-century writers are very revealing. An extreme example of a Whig historian is Thomas Babington Macaulay, whom Creighton both admired and disliked. Gibbon, he once observed,

took his stand upon the broad, substantial ground of the eighteenth century, upon its values – moral, intellectual, and artistic – of scepticism and urbanity, of moderation and harmony, of symmetry and balance. Macaulay's point of vantage was at once more exiguous and more impermanent. He was a complacent child of early nineteenth-century Whig politics and the early nineteenth-century Industrial Revolution. He was a Philistine, a materialist, a bigoted partisan, with an overemphatic debating style. As a political and social philosopher, he was damned; but what saved him was his high conception of the historian's vocation and his unflagging devotion to the art of narrative prose.[31]

What is significant about this passage is what is missing from it. Creighton has said nothing about Macaulay's notorious concept of progress; and he did not suspect that it might be related to the structuring effects of 'the art of narrative prose.'

Elsewhere, however, Creighton did refer to Macaulay's idea of progress. Macaulay, he observed, sided with the Whigs against the Tories. But a 'perhaps even more important aspect of [his] Whig Liberalism,' he continued, 'was his unquestioning belief in the reality of human progress. The Glorious Revolution was simply the beginning of an onward and upward climb which led straight to the glorious summit or zenith of the reign of Queen Victoria. Political advance, moral improvement, cultural refinement and material progress. *Above all, material progress.*'[32] Here he saw through Macaulay's idea of *inevitable* progress; but what he indicated was that historian's smug complacency, not the *linearity* of his thought. Noting that there was nothing Macaulay liked better than to point out to his readers the vast difference between a town, village, or district in the late seventeenth century and what it had become when he visited it in the first two decades of the reign of Queen Victoria, Creighton sided with Lytton Strachey who had called Macaulay 'a philistine, a man whose values are individualistic, vulgar, commonplace.'

It was not from Macaulay, however, but from another distinguished nineteenth-century Whig that Creighton took his concept of English- and French-Canadian social structures. For his interpretation comes straight out of Lord Durham's *Report on the Affairs of British North America* of 1839. It was Durham, not Creighton, who first conceived of English Canadians as embodying the progressive spirit of the age while the French Canadians remained 'an old and stationary society in a new and progressive world.' In all essentials they were still French, Durham observed, 'but French in every respect dissimilar to those of France in the present day. They resemble rather the French of the provinces under the old régime.'[33]

And so it happened that the novel communications theory of Innis became linked to an old concept of historical change at just about the time that concept was coming under attack by historians like Bury and Butterfield. That concept was a hidden assumption that underlay much of Creighton's thought. To remove such assumptions from one's own mind is more difficult than pulling teeth from one's own head; for one is unaware of them. To employ the language of Marshall McLuhan, these assumptions are part of the hidden *ground* upon which Creighton's interpretation appears as *figure*.

They are also cliché/archetypes. 'Archetypes,' observed Northrop Frye, 'are associative clusters, and differ from signs in being complex variables. Within the complex is often a large number of specific learned associations which are communicable because a large number of people in a given culture happen to be familiar with them.'[34] This definition can be applied to 'the Whig interpretation of history.' What Frye termed an archetype, McLuhan, it will be recalled, called a cliché. To be more precise, clichés, of which one is unconscious, become archetypes when they rise to consciousness. In the late 1920s and 1930s, when Creighton began to absorb some of the ideas of Innis, 'The Whig interpretation of history' was just beginning to be raised to consciousness by the work of historians like Bury and Butterfield.

V

Creighton's thought was also informed by an idiosyncratic literary bias. 'History differs from political science, economic theory, and sociology and also from philosophy,' he once explained,

not only and obviously in its subject matter, but also in its method, which is mainly narrative and descriptive rather than analytical and expository. History's closest affiliation is with literature: it is not a science, and is, or should be, a literary art or craft, and its most appropriate form is narrative. Narrative history represented by Gibbon, Macaulay, Froude, Trevelyan, Bryant, Runciman, and Taylor, is the main English tradition; and the historians who have had any influence on my work are almost exclusively British historians.[35]

One wonders what the Innis who criticized Sir James Jeans for separating physics from the category 'philosophy' would have made of the categories employed here. By Creighton's own definition, the essay from which the above quotation has been abstracted is not history, and apparently not literature either; for it is analytical and expository rather than narrative and descriptive. Why history should have more in common with literature than with other disciplines he did not explain. 'The writing of history' was separated in his mind from 'the study of history.' Of the historians who he indicated had influenced him, the first four belonged to the school assailed by Butterfield.*

---

* Butterfield attacked his contemporaries only indirectly, directing his aim at dead historians like Lord Acton. As John Kenyon observes: 'it was generally assumed when ... [*The Whig Interpretation*] was first published that it was directed chiefly at Trevelyan, together with his Whig predecessors Gardiner and Stubbs. Butterfield denied this more than once, but Trevelyan himself said it must refer to him, because he was "the last Whig historian in the world," and certainly Butterfield must have been singularly obtuse not to realize that most of his strictures were immediately applicable to his own regius professor.' (John Kenyon, *The History Men*, London 1983, 230).

Strictly speaking, Gibbon, it is true, wrote not of progress, but of a decline and fall of the Roman Empire; but that is merely a linearly inverted form of progress.

In his next paragraph Creighton qualified his initial assertions. To say that history was an art or craft did not mean that it could dispense with the disciplined and systematic procedures of the scientific method, and it must make careful use of the semi-scientific tools of the social sciences. But the use of scientific practice did not convert history into a science, 'not at least in the sense in which the word was used by the logical positivists. They believe that the business of history is the discovery and elucidation of general laws and universal truths, of which particular events are merely illustrations or examples.' So too, he might have added, did Harold Innis.

In his stand, Creighton allied himself with the so-called idealists, such as R.G. Collingwood and Michael Oakshott. 'Covering laws,' he continued, 'if they are really valid, are so vague and general that they illustrate nothing of interest. Historical events are unique and basically incomparable; and the only way to their understanding is to get beneath them into the human hopes, ideals, purposes and intentions by which they were inspired.' Here, having claimed that historical events are not comparable, he has dismissed all possibility of comparative history, which would include the work of the analogically minded Innis.

'History – the course of events that is –' Creighton continued, 'is an unending and bewildering torrent of multitudinous, unique facts.' The historian must choose from 'this vast, formless mass' elements 'he thinks essential to its understanding, and compose them in such a way as to reveal their meaning and significance, as he sees it. His task is selection and arrangement. His aim is pattern – the composite of the leading qualities or features of his period. His purpose is the discovery of the significant form or design which will reveal the essential meaning beneath the chaos of facts.' The implication here seems to be that the historian does not study data in relation to the ground, or context, in which they are embedded; rather he selects data from a meaningless chaos and imposes on them, or reads into them, a pattern.

Happily, Creighton did not invariably put this doctrine into practice. Indeed, he usually carefully compared data; and he did not always view them as being swept along in 'an unending and bewildering torrent' or as a 'chaos of facts' without contextual meaning. But he had a tendency to do so. Not with respect to particular details that fitted into his own categories of thought, about which he strove to be meticulously accurate; but with regard to large patterns of meaning alien to his understanding – the late work of Innis, for example – which he would re-order to impose his own *subjective* patterns of meaning. His interpretation of history was intensely subjective.

Creighton was influenced by Innis's communications studies only insofar as those studies related to transportation – to rivers, to canals, and to railroads. When he dealt with 'the commercial empire of the St. Lawrence' his approach apparently had been that of a North American-oriented materialist; and he had been an apologist for the material interests of the Montreal mercantile class. Indeed, concepts of American materialism then so informed his mind that he even treated that progressively minded, English, Whig aristocrat the Earl of Durham as a *convert* to an American, mercantile way of life. 'As the first great convert to the American gospel,' he wrote,

Durham was not concerned to give impartially equal treatment to artificial political units like Upper and Lower Canada; for he was thinking in terms of North America. He could not be fair to French Canada, for he was dreaming typically American dreams of expansion and prosperity.

The man's whole character – his optimism, restless energy and brusque aggressiveness – seems to sum up the spirit of a confident, questing, commercial generation. He could respond to America's way of life, he could see America's future; and this instinctive sympathy determines considerably the attitude, ideas and temper of the report.[36]

There is nonsense to be discovered in this passage; and it is most significant nonsense.

Creighton did not perceive that an English radical Whig aristocrat of the nineteenth century did not need to borrow a myth of progress from North American merchants, that the cliché/ archetype was part and parcel of the cultural baggage he carried up the St Lawrence from the old country. And, as Durham's report makes perfectly clear, he was not so much thinking 'in terms of North America' as in terms of the British Empire, to the maintenance of which his recommendations were addressed. Hence, whatever else may, or may not, have prevented him from being fair to French Canada, it was not because 'he was dreaming typically American dreams of expansion and prosperity.' Here, again, Creighton has shown remarkably little sense of figure/ground relations, of the English context from which he has abstracted the figure of Durham, and of the North American context within which he has placed it.

But we must also be aware of the context within which Creighton himself was writing. His view of 'progress' was then largely shared by the 'continentalist' and 'Liberal' schools of historical interpretation he was seeking to persuade or undermine. And this may well have been his reason for representing Durham as a convert to an American way of life. The American dream of Lord Durham, moreover, is a dream of Manifest Destiny and, however historically misleading, is important to any understanding of Donald Creighton, whose dream it truly was.

Creighton would later discover something very like this dream inspiring the politics of the Fathers of Confederation; especially those of Sir John A. Macdonald. It was Macdonald who, having taken a leading role in consolidating four British North American colonies into the Dominion of Canada in 1867, later, as the Dominion's prime minister, extended it to the Pacific coast, in part by promoting the building of the Canadian Pacific Railway, which extended the communications system of the St Lawrence. If one were to employ the language of Harold Innis, Macdonald, in contrast to certain opponents of his plans, gave expression to a bias of space, as did his biographer Donald Creighton.

VI

It will be recalled that Innis mistrusted written constitutions and that he viewed the centrist British North America Act with considerable suspicion. According to him, it had 'produced its own group of idolators and much has been done to interpret the views and sayings of the fathers of Confederation in a substantial body of patristic literature.'[37] Clearly, he did not intend to direct this stricture at Donald Creighton; but why he did not do so is quite unclear. Certainly after Innis's death it became more and more applicable; but even before that event Creighton's bias was evident.

It is impossible to examine all that historian's work in any detail here. It is instructive, however, to observe its development with respect to the British North America Act of 1867 and the Manitoba Act of 1870.

Creighton by no means entirely approved of the British North America Act, but this was for reasons directly opposed to those Innis had for disliking it. He thought it set up a regrettably decentralized form of government. 'With the utmost clarity and precision,' he observed, 'in speech after speech and resolution after resolution, the Fathers [of Confederation] set out their purpose of establishing a great transcontinental nation in the form of a constitutional monarchy under the British Crown.' It was true that their plan of union was flawed; but this was necessarily the case. 'Constitutional monarchy on the British model meant, of course, parliamentary sovereignty – the concentration of legislative power in a single sovereign legislature ...' Unfortunately, a federal arrangement had to be accepted. Legislative union was impossible 'partly because French Canada wished to guard its distinctive culture; and partly because the Maritime provinces, which had not developed municipal institutions, would have been left literally without any local government at all if their provincial legislatures had been abolished.'[38] The act, then, was a regrettable but intelligent political response to real political imperatives.

Initially Creighton thought of the Manitoba Act in the same way. In 1869, he explained, the Red River Colony was composed of Hudson's Bay Company officers, Canadian and American settlers, and English and French half-breeds. The French half-breeds,

the Métis, who hunted the buffalo, fought the Sioux Indians, and freighted goods for the Hudson's Bay Company, were the most politically conscious and effectively organized part of the community. They had a defiant sense of their own identity as a 'peculiar people' – a 'new nation'; and they and their clergy, the French missionary priests, were convinced that the distinctive Métis way of life would be threatened by the coming of a great mass of Protestant, English-speaking immigrants.[39]

Led by Louis Riel, the Métis seized control of the colony while Macdonald was negotiating its transfer from the Hudson's Bay Company. A provisional government was founded; a convention of French and English settlers decided upon terms of union with Canada and elected delegates to represent their views at Ottawa. Riel, the president of the provisional government, however, altered the list of rights the convention had accepted before it was presented at Ottawa.

Meanwhile Macdonald's government was seriously embarrassed. It had to please Catholic Quebec, which sympathized with the Métis; and it had to satisfy Protestant Ontario, which was outraged by the death of Thomas Scott, an Orangeman who had been executed by the Métis. Above all, it had to stop the trouble and complete the transfer of the territory to Canadian jurisdiction. 'The policy *which it wisely adopted* [emphasis mine],' Creighton concluded, 'combined the reality of conciliation with a show of force.'[40]

The show of force was the dispatch of Colonel Garnet Wolseley with a force of British regulars and Canadian militia. The policy of conciliation was the passage of the Manitoba Act. The territory would be united to Canada with the autonomy of a province; the English and French languages would be officially equal; Protestants and Catholics were to have separate schools.

Had Creighton come to see this conflict and its resolution by the light of the late work of Innis, he might have viewed the compromise embodied in the acts as the product of the collision of a society attempting to maintain itself in *time* with a centralized government attempting to extend its authority over *space*. He might also have thought it unfortunate that that compromise was cast in the form of a rigid statute that would plague Canadian politics for the next century. By reason of his linear concept of time, however, he thought of Innis's bewildering late work as irrelevant to Canadian history. And for the same reason he eventually came to view the Manitoba Act as anything but the outcome of wise policy.

This was because he became concerned with assailing a thesis known as 'the compact theory of Confederation,' which contended that Confederation had been an agreement between representatives of the English and French founding cultures and which he thought a threat to the political integrity of the country. With regard to the British North America Act this thesis could be attacked on the ground that it was the product of deliberations of delegates who, it could plausibly be argued, represented not cultures but regions, the old colonies of British North America. But with regard to the Manitoba Act this was not so clear. Indeed, here it could well be argued that, having been forced upon Macdonald by the Métis to the end of preserving their distinct culture, this act was indeed a compact.

In his last years Creighton launched many vigorous attacks upon contentions of this sort. Only one of these, however, need concern us here. Why did Macdonald accept the demands of the Métis, he once inquired: 'Why did he consent to impose such an elaborate constitution upon such an immature colony? How was he persuaded to settle all the basic institutions of a community which had not yet had time to develop its real and permanent character?'[41] This point of view differs little from that of Thomas Babington Macaulay. These are questions that surely could only be asked by a Whig historian. To assume that Manitoba was 'immature' in its early years as it was not in its later ones is like assuming that England was immature in the twelfth century as it was not when it had progressed to the nineteenth. And what did Creighton understand by 'the real and permanent character' of Manitoba? That province was surely no more lacking in reality to the Métis who lived there in 1870 than it was to their descendants a hundred years later; although the earlier reality may well have been more pleasant for them than some of the realities that succeeded it. Why, moreover, should one assume that Manitoba ever acquired a 'permanent character?' Creighton did not assume that Canada had acquired such a character; indeed, he very much feared it had not. That was the very reason he assailed the making of the Manitoba Act. Creighton ended his career as he began it, with a mind informed by 'Whig' concepts of history.

VII

Although other examples of the linear bias of Creighton's mind could be pointed to, one more will suffice for the purposes of this argument. McLuhan, it will be recalled, indicated that Innis's literary style resembled that of the modernists who emerged at the beginning of the twentieth century. Not even he, however, suggested that Innis wrote very well. It is therefore instructive to study Creighton's reaction to the work of a modernist who cast his thought into discontinuous, non-linear art forms and who unquestionably wrote very well indeed.

In his essay 'History and Literature,' Creighton remarks that novelists had taught him more about the art of narrative than historians and that he had been chiefly influenced by the great realistic novelists of the nineteenth and twentieth centuries, a common feature of whose work was 'a sensitive awareness of time.' As an example of this he pointed to Arnold Bennett's treatment of the death of Gerald Scales in *The Old Wives' Tale*, which he idiosyncratically related to T.S. Eliot's *The Waste Land*. 'It is a terrific scene,' he wrote with respect to Bennett's work,

in which Time seems to be physically present, just as he does, perhaps even more portentously, in the last lines of the second part of T.S. Eliot's *The Waste Land*. There the scene is a public house at closing time. The proprietor keeps calling out, 'Hurry up please, it's time, hurry up please, it's time.' And Time seems suddenly to stand in the doorway, a dreadful figure bidding the company begone. Time is the essence of history; and any young student who wants to be an historian and hasn't a sensitive feeling for time – for growth and change and decay – had better alter his plans and take up a timeless and lifeless study such as political science or economic theory.[42]

What Harold Innis, the political economist whose concern for time was only matched by his interest in space, might have made of the final comment, we shall never know; but the whole passage is clearly more informative with respect to the mind of Creighton than it is illuminating with regard to *The Waste Land*.

The personification of Time standing in the doorway bidding the company begone is not contained in the poem; it is an embellishment added by Creighton. He has recast, moreover, a discontinuous poem into narrative form by removing the pub scene from the context of the rest of the poem to impose his own meaning.

The Waste Land, which Creighton has interpreted diachronically, is essentially synchronic in that both time and space have been collapsed. The cockney cronies in the pub are juxtaposed with Elizabeth and Essex, Phlebis the Phoenician, one Stetson who seems to have fought on the ships at Mylae, and a host of others. Time is annihilated by Eliot. The persons and events alluded to in the poem are unified, not in time and space, but in the timeless consciousness of the seer Tiresias. As Eliot himself explained: 'Tiresias, although a mere spectator and not indeed a "character", is yet the most important personage in the poem, uniting all the rest. Just as the one-eyed merchant, seller of currants, melts into the Phoenician Sailor, and the latter is not wholly distinct from Ferdinand Prince of Naples, so all the women are one woman, and the two sexes meet in Tiresias. What Tiresias *sees*, in fact, is the substance of the poem.'[43] Thus personages and events are unified in the dreamlike consciousness of Tiresias or, more properly, in that of T.S. Eliot.

This juxtaposition resembles the juxtaposition of medieval German-speaking nuns, pagan Eskimos, and the American constitution unified in the consciousness of Innis. In contrast, for example, to the nonsensical juxtaposition of shoes and ships and sealing wax, of cabbages and kings, which were once unified in the consciousness of Lewis Carroll, the juxtapositions of Eliot and Innis make sense.

But they can never make sense when read diachronically.

Creighton did this when he read *The Waste Land* the way he read *The Old Wives' Tale* and imposed his concept of time upon Eliot. When he encountered the synchronic he attempted to make sense of it by translating it into the diachronic. His mind was governed by a temporal metaphor, a linear concept of time that expressed time in terms of space. To have come to terms with either the late work of Innis or the poetry of Eliot, he would have had to rid himself of this defective 'medium of communication.'

VIII

Creighton might have been able to do so had he rid himself of the notion that history '– the course of events that is – is an unending and bewildering torrent of multitudinous, unique facts' and applied his own Laurentian thesis. To have done this he could have called upon the resources of the social sciences, the usefulness of which he acknowledged, but which he held to be of secondary importance to imaginative fiction. In particular, he could have called upon the work of the American psychologist William James, who about 1890 had begun to write about a 'stream of consciousness.' This might have enabled him to see that the human mind is much like the St Lawrence River.

James's new metaphor enabled one to distinguish between the form and content of the mind, between the mind and the ideas that pass through it, in a way that is analogous to the way in which Innis had distinguished between the form and content of rivers. James was concerned to displace metaphors related to connected thought – such as 'chain of thought' or 'train of thought' – and to point out that ideas in the mind are not always serially related or logically and sequentially linked. 'Consciousness,' he wrote, ' ... does not appear to itself chopped up in bits. Such words as "chain" or "train" do not describe it fitly as it presents itself in the first instance. It is nothing jointed; it flows.

A "river" or a "stream" are the metaphors by which it is most naturally expressed.'[44]

James also likened the movement of ideas in the mind to that of a bird in flight, an alternation of flights and perchings. These perchings or resting places, writes a recent critic, 'are the substantive parts of thought, the places of flight are the transitive parts. James cares more for the transitive parts, the process of thinking, than for the substantive parts, the thoughts reached or defined; if only because, traditionally, philosophers and psychologists have hardly noticed the birds in flight, or adverted to the energy such flights discover and display.'[45] A very similar metaphor of a bird in flight, perching ever and anon, borrowed not from James but from Hegel, informed the mind of Harold Innis. In 'Minerva's Owl,' he wrote:

'Minerva's owl begins its flight only in the gathering dusk ...' Hegel wrote in reference to the crystallization of culture achieved in major classical writings in the period that saw the decline and fall of Grecian civilization. The richness of that culture, its uniqueness, and its influence on the history of the West suggest that the flight began not only for the dusk of Grecian civilization but also for the civilization of the West.[46]

'Since its flight from Constantinople,' he resumed some twenty-seven pages later, 'Minerva's owl has found a resting-place only at brief intervals in the West. It has flown from Italy to France, the Netherlands, Germany and after the French Revolution back to France and England and finally to the United States. These hurried and uncertain flights have left it little energy and have left it open to attack from numerous enemies.'[47] It is possible to argue that the flight of this metaphoric owl was entirely irrelevant to the rise and fall of civilizations; but it is not possible to argue that the bird's flight did not mirror a moving pattern – or flight – of ideas in the consciousness of Innis.

It is the metaphor of 'the stream of consciousness,' however, that chiefly concerns us here. It informed the poetry of T.S. Eliot and the novels of James Joyce. Neither writer appears to have had a significant influence upon Donald Creighton; but both profoundly affected Marshall McLuhan, whose work united their thought with that of Innis.

IX

Suspended from a wall of the nineteenth-century carriage house from which McLuhan directed the Centre for the Study of Technology and Culture at the University of Toronto was a chart representing the commonly accepted Shannon-Weaver mathematical model of communication. McLuhan in no way agreed with this diagram; indeed he used it only to illustrate what he took to be most misleading in orthodox communications theory.

The Shannon-Weaver model represented a *message* passing *linearly* from an *information source* to a *transmitter*. From thence it again proceeded *linearly* as a *signal* to a *receiver* to pass, again as a *message*, to its *destination*. Connected to this model, interrupting communications between transmitter and receiver, was a *noise source*. As explained by Warren Weaver,

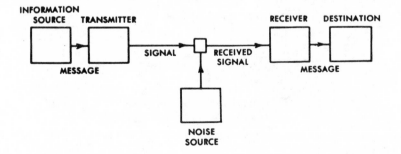

The *information source* selects a desired *message* out of a set of possible messages ... The selected message may consist of written or spoken words, or of pictures, music, etc.

The *transmitter* changes this *message* into the *signal* which is actually sent over the *communication channel* from the transmitter to the *receiver*. In the case of telephony, the channel is a wire, the signal a varying electrical current on this wire; the transmitter is the set of devices (telephone transmitter, etc.) which change the sound pressure of the voice into the varying electrical current. In telegraphy, the transmitter codes written words into sequences of interrupted currents of varying lengths (dots, dashes, spaces). In oral speech, the information source is the brain, the transmitter is the voice mechanism producing the varying sound pressure (the signal) which is transmitted through the air (the channel). In radio the channel is simply space ... and the signal is the electromagnetic wave which is transmitted.[48]

In the process of transmission, Weaver further explains, 'it is unfortunately characteristic that certain things are added to the signal which were not intended by the information source. These unwanted additions may be distortions of sound (in telephony, for example) or static (in radio), or distortions in shape or shading of picture (television), or errors in transmission (telegraphy or facsimile), etc. All of these changes in transmitted signal are called noise.'

'This theory is so general,' Weaver later continued,

that one does not need to say what kinds of symbols are being considered – whether written letters or words, or musical notes, or spoken words, or symphonic music, or pictures. The theory is deep enough so that the relationships it reveals indiscriminately apply to other forms of communication. This means, of course, that the theory is sufficiently imaginatively motivated so that it is dealing with the real inner core of the communications problem, no matter what special form the actual case may take.[49]

Thus Weaver contended, the theory had a universal applicability.

McLuhan had two major objections to this model. First, he insisted that noise was part of the communication process; second, he observed that this model took no account of figure/ground relations. Weaver and Shannon, he contended, had something like a pipeline in mind, a container that might transport oil from one place to another but that could also have side effects upon a ground, or environment, of which their model took no account. He put it this way:

What they [Shannon and Weaver] call 'NOISE,' I call the *medium* – that is, all the side-effects, all the unintended patterns and changes. Their model is from the telegraph which they see merely as a kind of pipeline for transportation. Recently, while debating the Alaska oil pipeline here in Canada, it was brought out vividly that it would destroy the indigenous peoples, in all directions. The Shannon/Weaver model of communication is merely a transportation model which has no place for the side-effects of the service environments ... For example, the motor car is not a medium but a *figure* in a *ground* of services, i.e., highways, factories, oil companies, etc. It is always the service environment that is the medium, and this is usually 'hidden' in the sense of being unnoticed. Thus all media tend to be subliminal in their structures, and this I have been trying to say in the phrase 'the medium is the message,' i.e., the *effects* of all media manifest its [*sic*] form, and the effects are hidden.[50]

To these objections of McLuhan it is possible to add two more. The mathematical theory of Shannon and Weaver, so far from being universally applicable, takes no account of activities such as those of the historian. For the study of history, as distinguished from the writing of the same, is not an act of transmission but one of retrieval. Furthermore, to the historian the absence of data is frequently as significant as its presence, the hidden context as important as the evident. In other words the historian can be as interested in what is not being mediated by a communications system as in what is. He can also be very interested in noise, or what has been mediated in distorted form.

This chapter has been concerned with all these things, with Innis and Creighton considered as receivers and transmitters, with what was received and what was rejected, and with noise. Above all, it has been concerned with contexts. The model that best seems to fit these data is that of McLuhan.

FOUR

ARCHETYPAL CRITICISM

I

When Marshall McLuhan with Wilfred Watson published *From Cliché to Archetype* in 1970 it was not very widely reviewed and the critics who did consider it were for the most part either hostile or uninformed. One irritated reviewer, the novelist John Fowles, observed that, while it was said that the book had taken ten years to write, it was

as elegant and lucid as a barrel of tar, it makes one wonder whether Marshall McLuhan's celebrated doubts over the print medium don't largely stem from a personal incapacity to handle it. Perhaps the graceless style, the barbarously obscuring jargon, the incoherent hopping from one unfinished argument into the middle of the next are all meant to be subtly humorous. But the general effect is about as subtle and humorous as a Nazi storm trooper hectoring the latest trainload of Jews ... There is a late reference to 'pestilential linguistic smog,' and many who have struggled through the dense, polluted sentences of the text will see the phrase as more of a boomerang than an outward-flying barb.[1]

McLuhan, having chosen not to write his book linearly and sequentially, had ordered it discontinuously and alphabetically, after the fashion of a dictionary, by the first letter of the chapter titles. The 'Introduction' thereby began on page 116, falling between a chapter entitled 'Identity – the Culture Hero' and another headed 'Jokes.' Fowles was unamused. 'I don't find this jumbling very original or witty,' he wrote. 'Like so many of the professors' ... aphorisms and word-plays, the gimmick has maximum built-in obsolescence.'

'The argument of the book,' Fowles discovered, 'is that from the debris of exhausted clichés (not only verbal but technological, social, artistic, etc. – the term is expanded, stretched beyond endurance, to cover any "retrievable" human phenomenon) man derives the material from which he forms his new, contemporary clichés. The old clichés become archetypes, and are then reassembled and re-clichéified in their turn. In plain English, most of today is yesterday rehashed.' This basic thesis Fowles found to be 'something of a platitude itself.'

Many readers of *From Cliché to Archetype*, which assuredly is not easy to assimilate, might well agree with Fowles's assessment. More cautious critics, however, might recall that not-too-dissimilar criticism might easily, if imprudently, be directed at a good deal of McLuhan's own favourite reading matter; at *Finnegans Wake* for example, a passage from which, along with his own exegesis, McLuhan published in the eccentrically located introduction. There he observed that in treating the theme of cliché and archetype in relation to printing, James Joyce was not only discussing the subject 'but *illustrating* [emphasis mine] the linguistic means for tackling it on several levels at once.'[2] In treating the same theme, McLuhan was doing much the same thing. His 'introduction,' moreover, may be read as a *ground* upon which the rest of the book appears as *figure*; and vice versa.

In considering *From Cliché to Archetype*, a reader should recall McLuhan's much more successful book, *Understanding Media: The Extensions of Man*. There he had written:

A fairly complete handbook for studying the extensions of man could be made up from selections from Shakespeare. Some might quibble about whether or not he was referring to TV in these familiar lines from *Romeo and Juliet*:

> But soft! what light through yonder window breaks?
> It speaks, and yet says nothing.[3]

Critics of the book pounced upon this passage. To some it was preposterous to suppose that Shakespeare could know anything about television; others pointed out that the quotation was not exact. In the introduction to the second edition, McLuhan observed: 'On page 27 there are some lines from Romeo and Juliet whimsically modified to make an allusion to TV. Some reviewers have imagined that this was an involuntary misquotation.'[4] That was all. McLuhan's critics might have rejoined that he had botched things again; that the quotation appeared not on page 27 but on page 25. To have done so, however, would have been to have again missed the point. McLuhan was *demonstrating* that the medium is the message, the medium here being a metaphor the content of which could shift. He did not, however, directly point this out to his critics; to have done so would have been to destroy a teaching device.

In thinking about the form of *From Cliché to Archetype*, and the prose McLuhan employed in it, it is helpful to recall a comparison he once made between the prose of T.S. Eliot and that of Erza Pound. Eliot, he observed, confined his discontinuities and abrupt juxtapositions to his poetry. He had 'held the interest of a whole generation of readers by making basic concessions in his prose to their demand for dialectical and persuasive charm. What he has to say, however, is neither dialectical nor charming, but profoundly analogical and even unpleasant.'[5] But Pound, whose poetry and prose had been influenced by the structure of the Chinese ideogram, made no such concession. Pound had observed that Eliot's *Sweeney Agonistes* contained more essential criticism of Seneca than Eliot's essay on English Senecanism. This was not a casual statement, McLuhan observed,

but an ideogram, a presentation of an analogical proportion depending on a precise analysis of Seneca, on the one hand, and of *Sweeney Agonistes*, on the other. Syntactically elaborated it would fill many pages. But Mr. Pound seldom translates himself into ordinary prose. And anecdotes and reported conversations which enrich his essays are, in the same way, never casually illustrative but ideogrammatic. In the language of the schoolmen, for whose precision of dissociation Mr.

Pound has so frequently expressed his admiration, the ideogram represents the 'copula of agglutination.' That is to say, the copula which connects enunciations and conceptions in rationalistic discourse. And it is the consequent solidity and sharpness of particularized actuality (in which the Chinese excel) that baffles the reader who looks for continuous argumentation in Mr. Pound's prose and verse alike.[6]

In considering *From Cliché to Archetype* one must judge whether its author was a failed Eliot, or an uncompromising Pound, or neither. One might conclude that what Fowles took particular exception to was McLuhan's 'ideogrammatic' prose style.

Another reader of the book, the literary critic Hugh Kenner, a leading authority on Eliot, Pound, and Joyce, and well acquainted with McLuhan, was perceptive and witty, but unimpressed. Kenner took note of the book's structure. He observed that the alphabetical arrangement of the chapters was a 'Gutenburg device' designed to keep anyone from looking for sequential argument; but he thought it a failure. 'A book curved round on itself like this has, like the round earth, a great potential for internal tensions. Alas, not being really *written*, only spilled out, it misses such opportunities, and the author's belief that it is "his most important work since 'Understanding Media' " remains only potentially true.'[7] He contended that McLuhan's discontinuities were too weak. Tension, it appeared, operates grandly between 'points of emphatic compression,' as between the earth and the moon, 'but only minimally between the atoms in a spilled sea.' McLuhan's work was like a spilled sea. Shifting to an electric metaphor, Kenner remarked: 'A voltage is a difference, as between ground and cloud. No art can step up the voltage of boiled spinach, whatever its nutritive power.' It was a pity, he thought, that 'with much insight glimpsing around inside it ... many readers are going to call the book spinach, and then go on to quote the rest of the famous cliché.'*

* The reference is to a well-known cartoon in the *New Yorker* magazine (see

'It's broccoli, dear.'
'I say it's spinach, and I say the hell with it.'

Drawing by Carl Rose; © 1928, 1956, The New Yorker Magazine, Inc.

In treating the book's content, Kenner found it no less trite than had Fowles. Observing that, according to McLuhan, yesterday's cliché was today's archetype, and that this was 'a classier name, to emphasize the fact that the obsolete, when it is rediscovered, is apt to be invested with class,' he continued:

Decades after the Victorian Novel became a hopeless cliché, John Fowles made the best-seller lists by crafting a Victorian novel.

The reason we pay for 'The French Lieutenant's Woman' instead of fetching a Victorian novel down from the attic is that John Fowles knows things about the Victorian novel that Victorian novelists didn't

---

above). The content of 'spinach,' like that of 'communications,' 'responsible government,' 'the St Lawrence River' and the rest, appears to have shifted.

know. His conscious attention – hence his book's show of psychological insight – is precisely on what his forerunners did unconsciously. So did Joyce labor, to simulate the clichés of his year's yesteryear (and Wyndham Lewis saw just half the point when he dismissed Stephen Dedalus as a cliché). So the Van Gogh faker knows things about Van Gogh's methods Van Gogh couldn't have told us, and might be better rewarded did not a powerful interest in Van Gogh regulate our system of approvals.

It seemed clear to Kenner 'that "archetype" – like most McLuhan terms: one remembers "medium" – is a dog's coat to gather whatever burrs it touches. ... doubtless one can argue on behalf of most McLuhan connections, though McLuhan characteristically doesn't argue. He simply asserts.'

If one could 'argue on behalf of most McLuhan connections,' it follows that it was not altogether necessary for him to have done so himself. And this suggests the possibility that he intended his readers to engage in just such an argument. And, if this were the case, what Kenner termed 'assertions' might be read as 'illustrations.' Fowles deemed McLuhan's connections more dubious than did Kenner; but in one respect he may better, if reluctantly, have perceived what McLuhan was up to. 'McLuhan,' he wrote, 'belongs ... to the machine-gun school of pundits. He sprays so many assertions at so many targets that some are bound to hit the mark. A lot more are equally bound to miss. A kinder reviewer might call this book provocative.'

A kinder reviewer might have been right. To be provocative in this manner, to 'involve' the mind of a reader with a medium of communication by way of discontinuities, was what McLuhan termed 'cool.' In any event, to have been at all provocative the book would have had to have been considerably less old hat and banal than Fowles previously contended. But again we must note that here Kenner was in agreement with him; the book was a failed attempt at archetypalizing *Understanding Media*, at archetypalizing, that is to say, clichés.

McLuhan, it will be argued below, was not simply firing off rounds of unsubstantiated assertions. In his own peculiar fashion he was engaged in a long sustained argument as to the nature of the cliché/archetype. He was also engaged in a subsidiary argument with his colleague Northrop Frye. His argument was non-linear and non-sequential; and to perceive it fully one must examine the *ground* upon which *From Cliché to Archetype* appeared as *figure* and take careful note of the book's odd structure.

II

As late as 1933, when the 'corrected reissue' of the *Oxford English Dictionary* was published, the word 'archetype' was defined as 'the original pattern or model from which copies are made, a prototype.' Beyond this, the term was assigned just two secondary meanings. In minting, an archetype was 'a coin of standard weight by which others are adjusted'; and in comparative anatomy it was 'an assumed ideal pattern of the fundamental structure of each great division of organized being of which the various species are considered as manifestations.' That was all.

In 1972, when the *Supplement to the Oxford English Dictionary* was published, the inadequacy of these entries was recognized. Two further definitions were added. One of these pertained to the archetypes of the collective unconscious as employed in the analytical psychology of Carl Jung. The other related to the term as it had come to be used in the literary criticism of Maud Bodkin and Northrop Frye. In neither Jung's nor Bodkin's nor Frye's usage was the term synonomous with 'prototype.'

Over the years, 'archetype' has denoted a variety of differing concepts. It has commonly been used with reference to the ideal forms of Plato. Beyond this, as Jung observed, it

occurs as early as Philo Judaeus, with reference to the *Imago Dei* (God-image) in man. It can also be found in Irenaeus, who says: 'The creator of the world did not fashion these things directly from himself but copied them from archetypes outside himself.' In the *Corpus Hermeticum*, God is called ... (archetypal light). The term occurs several times in Dionysius, the Areopagite, as for instance in *De caelesti hierarchia* ... 'immaterial Archetypes,' and in *De divinis nominibus* ... 'Archetypal stone.' The term 'archetype' is not found in St. Augustine, but the idea of it is. Thus in *De diversis quaestionibus* LXXXIII he speaks of 'ideae principales' 'which are themselves not formed ... but are contained in the divine understanding.'[8]

More recently the term was used by John Locke to signify 'one of the external realities with which our ideas and impressions to some extent correspond.'[9] And in this century the expression has been interestingly used by André Gide. 'Est-ce que le Savant fair rien d'autre?' he inquired. 'Lui aussi,' he continued, 'recherche l'archétype des choses et les lois de leur succession; il recompose un monde enfin, idéalement simple, où tout s'ordonne normalement.'[10] Doubtless the term has had yet other usages that cannot be noticed here.

Although Jung's theory of archetypes developed in stages,[11] the Oxford dictionary definition of his concept – 'a pervasive idea, image or symbol that forms part of the collective unconscious' – is somewhat misleading; for Jung distinguished between archetypes, which being part of the unconscious are of unknown form, and the archetypal ideas, images, and symbols to which they give rise in consciousness. In Jungian psychology the archetypes themselves are the most fundamental ingredients of the psyche; they are the forms that underlie everything we perceive, imagine, and think.

By the word 'archetype' Northrop Frye did not mean what Jung meant by the term; nor did his concept coincide with those of all other literary archetypalists. It did not coincide, for example, with that of Maud Bodkin, the only other student of literature quoted by the Oxford dictionary. Greatly influenced by Jung, she had published *Archetypal Patterns in Poetry: Psychological Studies of Imagination* in 1934. As Frye himself once remarked: 'because I found the term "archetype" an essential one, I am still often called a Jungian critic, and classified with Miss Maud Bodkin, whose book I have read with interest, but whom, on the evidence of that book, I resemble about as closely as I resemble the late Sarah Bernhardt.'[12] And Frye's notion of the archetype differs from those of more recent scholars than Bodkin; from that of the historian of religions, Mircea Eliade, for example, or from that of Joseph Campbell, the student of comparative mythology.

Campbell's understanding of the term would seem to have been essentially that of Jung;[13] that of Eliade, however, was different. As he explained in the Torchbook (Harper and Row) edition of *Cosmos and History*, for Jung archetypes were structures of the collective unconscious; but in his own book he nowhere touched 'upon problems of depth psychology nor do I use the concept of the collective unconscious ... I use the term "archetype," ... as a synonym for "exemplary model" or "paradigm," that is, in the last analysis, in the Augustinian sense.'[14] But for Eliade the term was not synonymous with just any exemplary model or paradigm.

Following Beverly Moon's summary of Eliade's thought, archetypes provided models of institutions and norms of behaviour for a member of tribal and traditional cultures; they constituted a sacred reality revealed to mankind at the beginning of time. Consequently, the archetypal patterns are regarded as having had a supernatural or transcendent origin.

These observations provide the basis for Eliade's description of the way in which religious man distinguishes two separate modes of being in the world: the sacred and the profane. The member of a tribal or traditional society may be called *homo religiosus* ('religious man') precisely because he perceives both a transcendent model (or archetype) and a mundane reality that is capable of being molded to correspond to the transcendent model. Furthermore, he experiences the transcendent model as holy, that is, as manifesting absolute power and value. In fact it is the sacred quality of the archetype that compels him to orient his life around it. Finally, the sacred is recognized as such because it appears to man within the profane setting of everyday events. This is the hierophany ('appearance of the sacred'), that is, when the supernatural makes itself felt in all its numinosity in contrast to the natural order.[15]

It should be noted, however, that Eliade did not think of his usage as being contradictory of that of Jung; it was merely different from Jung's.

It was not entirely different, however, for in Eliade's view 'the archetypal patterns linger on in the unconscious of modern man, serving as themes that motivate and guide him ... On the individual level, the person may play out an unconsciously motivated role that has a recognizable mythical form: the hero, the sacred marriage, the wise old woman, the eternal child. The paradigms appear in numerous constellations with varied force at different times, even during the life of the individual.'[16]

Account must also be taken of the literary use of the archetype as explored by Lauriat Lane, who attempted to unite Frye's thought with that of Maud Bodkin and other critics.[17] Lane observed that the first literary critic to make use of the term in its modern sense was Samuel Johnson. 'If mankind were left to judge for themselves,' wrote Johnson, 'it is reasonable to imagine, that of such writings, at least, as describe the movements of the human passions, and of which every man carries the archetype within him, a just opinion would be formed.' Johnson, according to Lane, established the fact that the major importance of archetypes lies in their universality, a fact that provides a way by which detailed analysis of a literary work can lead directly to the largest possible view of literature and its functions. Lane then pointed to 'a counter-position of romantic subjectivism' that considered what went on in the mind of the reader. Charles Lamb, in his essay 'Witches and Other Night Fears,' had written: 'Gorgons, and Hydras, and Chimaeras dire – stories of Celaeno and the Harpies – may reproduce themselves in the brain of superstition – but they were there before. They are transcripts, types – the archetypes are in us, and eternal. How else should the recital of that, which we know in a waking sense to be false, come to affect us at all?' Lamb, Lane contended, here implied what later became essential in Jung's psychological formulation of the term, that the workings of the archetype within the human mind take place on something other than a conscious and rational level of apprehension.

According to Lane, one of the first examples of direct archetypal criticism is to be discovered in Gilbert Murray's essay 'Hamlet and Orestes,' in which Murray reached conclusions similar to those of Jung, but independently of him. 'Murray's perceptions and interpretations,' wrote Lane, 'are all the more valuable for being arrived at by way of a careful and imaginative literary analysis and comparison rather than a reading of Jung. His description of the archetypal situation as "a great unconscious solidarity and continuity, lasting from age to age, among all the children of the poets, both the makers and the callers-forth, both the artists and the audiences," more than atones for a certain vagueness of language by its freedom from excessive psychological jargon.'

Lane then quoted from Jung's essay 'On the Relation of Analytical Psychology to Creative Art.' The primordial image or archetype, Jung had written, 'is a figure, whether it be daemon, man, or process, that repeats itself in the course of history wherever creative fantasy is fully manifested. Essentially, therefore, it is a mythological figure. If we subject these images to a closer investigation, we discover them to be the formulated resultants of countless typical experiences of our ancestors.

They are, as it were, the psychic residua of numberless experiences of the same type.' The best application of Jung's theories to literary study, Lane maintained, was Maud Bodkin's *Archetypal Patterns in Poetry* wherein she united Jung's terminology with Murray's approach to literature to provide 'the best possible literary definition of archetypes in terms of the psychology of the reader.'

The outstanding advocate of archetypal criticism at the present time (1954), wrote Lane, was Northrop Frye. His most basic contribution to archetypal criticism was his stated desire for 'a co-ordinating principle, a central hypothesis' behind which must lie 'the assumption of total coherence.' Of almost equal importance was Frye's reminder of two possible approaches in archetypal criticism. 'We may ... proceed inductively from structural analysis,' Frye had written, 'associating the data we collect and trying to see larger patterns in them. Or we may proceed deductively, with the consequences that follow from postulating the unity of criticism.' Frye had also defined the place of anthropology, exemplified in the work of Sir James Fraser, in archetypal criticism. The search for archetypes, he had written, 'is a kind of literary anthropology, concerned with the way that literature is informed by pre-literary categories such as ritual, myth and folk tale.'

Lane then attempted to move beyond Frye and his predecessors. Among all the critics he had discussed, only Jung had devoted himself at any length to the creative process. His distinction between the extravertive and the introvertive writer was central to the problem, a distinction that Lane held to be an entirely valid contribution to literary psychology. Of the extravertive writer's works, Jung had observed:

These works positively impose themselves upon the author; his hand is, as it were, seized, and his pen writes things that his mind perceives with amazement. The work brings with it its own form; what he would add to it is declined, what he does not wish to admit is forced upon him. While his consciousness stands disconcerted and empty before the phenomenon, he is overwhelmed with a flood of thoughts and images which it was never his aim to beget, and which his will would never have fashioned ... He can only obey and follow the apparently foreign impulse, feeling that his work is greater than himself, and therefore has a power over him that he is quite unable to command ...

Of the introvertive writer's writings, Jung had written:

These are works that proceed wholly from the author's intention and resolve to produce this or that effect. In this case the author submits his material to a definite treatment that is both directed and purposeful; he adds to it and subtracts from it, emphasizing one effect, modifying another, laying on this colour here, that there, with the most careful weighing of their possible effects, and with constant observance of the laws of beautiful form and style. To this labour the author brings his keenest judgement, and selects his expression with the most complete freedom. In his view his material is only material, and entirely subject to his artistic purposes; he wills to present this and nothing else.

This distinction, Lane observed, 'is primarily one of form and content. As Jung himself says, "the introverted attitude is characterized by an upholding of the subject [the author] with his conscious ends and aims against the claims and pretensions of the object; the extraverted attitude is distinguished by a subordination of the subject to the claims of the object." ' Lane thought that this made clear the difference between Jane Austen, who achieved technical perfection within the consciously limited world of her novels, and Charles Dickens, whose ambitious fictional projects always threatened to get out of hand. It was this that G.K. Chesterton had meant when he spoke of those critics who 'feel that Dickens is a great writer even if he is not a good writer.'

Finally Lane attempted his own definition of the literary archetype, which he developed from the point of view of the reader rather than of the author. The best critical work had been done by critics who were also creative artists; but they had failed to communicate their insights because they presented them from a point of view difficult or even impossible for the average reader, who was not himself a creative writer, to share.

The literary archetype, according to Lane, had five characteristics, whether one accepted Jung's hypothesis of a collective unconscious or ascribed all archetypal phenomena to tradition. First, it exhibits relative universality in time and space. Second, it has a traditional basis in literature and/or pre-literature. Third, it is possessed of innate significance of form and content. Fourth, the archetypal situation is always characterized by subconscious elements in author, work, and reader. Fifth, the most important quality of the archetype is that it arouses in the reader an emotional intensity at the moment of awareness.

Northrop Frye conceived of the archetype in a much more limited fashion. He defined it as 'a symbol, usually an image, which recurs often enough in literature to be recognizable as an element of one's literary experience as a whole'[18] and as 'a recurring or repeating unit, normally an image, which indicates that a poet is following a certain convention or working in a certain GENRE.'[19]

As we have earlier remarked, McLuhan, although making use of other people's definitions, never himself precisely defined what he meant by 'archetype.' His term 'cliché/archetype' in one way or another, however, might seem to comprehend a good many of the above-mentioned usages. As Kenner remarked, McLuhan's term resembles a dog's coat gathering burrs. But what distinguished his concept of archetype from all others was its relationship to cliché. The title of his book, McLuhan once explained to a reader, refers to a perfectly natural process in all human experience, private or corporate. It is the process by which we store any kind of experience for further use. To codify, or capsulate, or to record any experience whatever, we have to translate it into some other material. Language, as such, is a record of human perception. We are most aware of this in everyday slang, since it is that part of a speech which is most inductive to new perception. When we say 'I like mine barefoot', meaning 'I take my coffee without cream or sugar', we are translating into a single word a complicated set of perceptions, plus the *effect* that these have upon us. After a while, we can retrieve, or recall this effect by simply repeating 'barefoot' as *figure* against the *ground* of coffee. The frequent use of this word will diminish the effect it had at first. It will gradually become a cliché like 'getting the breaks', which is a term in music. After this expression shall become 'dead' cliché, it may linger in the subconscious depths of the language until suddenly revived by some encounter with another expression. When restored and brought back to new life, it may appear as a shining new archetype. The word 'barefoot' itself is an old cliché here being restored to vitality by a new context of 'coffee'.[20]

McLuhan was discussing live and dead metaphor in a way that certainly was not peculiar to him. 'In all discussion of m.[etaphor],' Fowler's *Dictionary of Modern English Usage* observes,

it must be borne in mind that some metaphors are living, i.e., are offered & accepted with a consciousness of their nature as substitutes for their literal equivalents, while others are dead, i.e., have been so often used that speaker & hearer have ceased to be aware that the words used are not literal; but the line of distinction between the live & the dead is a shifting one, the dead being sometimes liable, under the stimulus of an affinity or a repulsion, to galvanic stirrings indistinguishable from life.[21]

Beyond this, however, McLuhan applied the rules that governed metaphor to media of communication other than language.

Clichés, McLuhan explained, were revived by banging them into other clichés. Environments, he continued, were clichés; they were clichés hidden from us by sheer surround. 'In such surrounds, or all-enveloping situations, most people see the "content" or the *figure* rather than the *ground* in which the figure is placed. A fish may see other fish but never see water.'

III

Some of what McLuhan and his collaborator, Wilfred Watson, were up to is revealed in their private correspondence. In the summer of 1964 Watson wrote about treating media as dead metaphor. A medium was the message, he suggested, only for new media because then it was a metaphor. But for old, worn media certain rules had to be devised and followed to restore metaphoric force. These rules were what were called artists' forms. But media when worn have memories. And '*nota bene* this extension of the media-theory leads directly to clichés and archetypes which are the *memories* of the worn media. To treat the cliché/archetype complex in this way,' he continued, 'would both give it the force of your work on media and it would re-inforce that work too? [*sic*] It would take the cliché/archetype discussion out of the realm of Frye? [*sic*]' (and added in pencil 'into area of Joyce').[22] 'I agree with you entirely,' McLuhan replied, 'about the strategy of taking over the Frye world of literary genres via media as metaphors. However, in terms of capture, the Frye audience is opposed to the Frye field, the concept and title "Cliché to Archetype" may prove very effective. Actually we are not really engaged in the conquest of the Frigean empire so much as in the discovery of a totally new empire.'[23] This clearly indicates that the book contained fundamental arguments that escaped the attention of its critics, one of which was an argument about 'genres.' This argument was directed at Northrop Frye.

McLuhan distinguished between the novel perceptions of the 'artist' and the work of the archetypal critic Frye. 'It is Frye's peculiarity,' he wrote privately, 'that he can cope only with the Emperor's old clothes. This he calls archetypes. The Emperor's new clothes, that which is new and environmental, he ignores. It is this environmental world that is the concern of the artist. He tidies it up. He probes, and patterns, and shapes it. Archetypal critic, Mr. Frye, classifies the work of the artist.'[24] The conventional literary mind,' McLuhan contended, 'naturally tries to "connect" and to classify mythic and symbolic materials by reduction of oral to visual forms of order,' in support of which he quoted the anthropologist Edward Carpenter, an authority upon the Inuit.[25]

[Robert] Graves ... has 'corrected' Greek mythology in two volumes, eliminating contradictions, adding omissions, arranging lineally, and generally 'straightening out.' What I am getting at is that they first turn these myths into what they are not; by arranging symbols they create 'content'; then they pigeon-hole these various 'contents' and come up with archetypes. None of this interests me save the fact that, like Frye, they direct their attention towards a most important problem and, like a hedgehog, build humourless, water-tight systems ... that, instead of answering the problem or even illuminating it, block access to it.

Environmental blindness according to McLuhan, however, was not peculiar to Frye and Graves. 'The inability of [Ernst] Cassirer and [Carl] Jung to notice the interplay between myths, percepts, concepts, and technologies,' he argued, 'is itself a major testimony to the power of the environmental body to render itself invisible. Cassirer extends the idea of symbolic form to all the arts and sciences alike. [James] Joyce is certainly the only person who began to observe their meshing with technologies.'[26]

IV

There is an argument in *From Cliché to Archetype* unnoticed by the book's critics. The 'Introduction' begins with a discussion of a reversal of the roles of cliché and archetype between the ancient and the modern worlds. To archaic man language was an immediate evoker of reality, 'a magical form.' The idea that words merely correspond to reality is characteristic of highly literal societies in which the visual sense is dominant. 'Today,' McLuhan contended, 'in the age of quantum mechanics, for which the "chemical bond" is, according to Heisenberg and Linus Pauling and others, a "resonance," it is perfectly natural to resume a "magical" attitude to language. The poetry of statement became the crux of one of the great critical upheavals of the twentieth century. The change corresponds to the discovery that consciousness is also a multileveled event with its roots in the "deepest terrors and desires." '[27] It is important at this point to take note of a crucial difference between the thought of McLuhan and that of Innis. A governing metaphor in the thought of the latter, it was contended in the last chapter, was a concept of the space-time continuum borrowed from Einstein. This particular idea seems to have had little or no influence on the thinking of McLuhan. Outside of his introductions to Innis's work, he took no interest in biases of space or of time. But he did take other models from twentieth-century science. It was not the 'continuum' but the 'interval,' and the 'resonance' to which it gives rise, that concerned him. His metaphors derive from Heisenberg and Pauling. These he related to the work of the symbolists and the modernists.

The phrase 'deepest terrors and desires,' quoted by McLuhan

above, has to do with resonance. It is from an essay on Ben
Jonson by T.S. Eliot, who himself was part of 'one of the great
critical upheavals of the twentieth century.' 'If we look,' wrote
Eliot, 'at the work of Jonson's great contemporaries, Shakespeare, and also Donne and Webster, and Tourneur (and sometimes Middleton), have a depth a third dimension ... which
Johnson's work has not. Their words have often a network
of tentacular roots reaching down to the deepest terrors and
desires.'[28] The critical upheaval, within which Eliot worked, was
a psychological as well as a literary upheaval.

As we meditate upon the ancient clichés, McLuhan continued,
'the literal man is inclined to consider them as "archetypes."
For example, Northrop Frye in *Anatomy of Criticism* defines
archetype as "a symbol, usually an image, which recurs often
enough in literature to be recognizable as an element of one's
literary experience as a whole." Of course this particular definition is most unJungian in suggesting that archetypes are human
artifacts produced by much repetition – in other words, a form
of cliché.'[29] Frye would likely have agreed that in this respect his
thought was unJungian. For the psychologist, he had written, all
dream symbols are private ones, interpreted by the personal
life of the dreamer; but for the critic there is no such thing as
private symbolism, 'or, if there is, it is his job to make sure it
does not remain so.'

This problem is already present in Freud's treatment of *Oedipus Tyran-
nus* as a play which owes much of its power to the fact that it dramatizes
the Oedipus complex. The dramatic and psychological elements can
be linked without any reference to the personal life of Sophocles, of
which we know nothing whatever. This emphasis on impersonal content has been developed by Jung and his school, where the communica-
bility of archetypes is accounted for by a theory of a collective
unconscious – an unnecessary hypothesis in literary criticism, so far as
I can judge.[30]

A theory of a collective unconscious, however, although probably arrived at independently of Jung, informed both the poetry and literary criticism of T.S. Eliot.*

McLuhan also criticized a self-referential aspect of Frye's criticism. 'For the literary archetypalist,' he wrote, 'there is always a problem of whether *Oedipus Rex* or *Tom Jones* would have the same effect on an audience in the South Sea Islands as in Toronto.'[31] Here again he was concerned with figure/ground relationships.

V

The rest of *From Cliché to Archetype* may be read as an argument in support of, or as at least congruent with, the position staked out above. While the argument of the book cannot be pursued in great detail here, it is instructive to notice some further differences separating McLuhan and Frye. Take, for example, the chapter entitled 'Genres' in which Frye's thought is directly probed.

The critical theory of genres, Frye had observed,

is stuck precisely where Aristotle left it. The very word 'genre' sticks out in an English sentence as the unpronounceable and alien thing it is. Most critical efforts to handle such generic terms as 'epic' and 'novel' are chiefly interesting as examples of the psychology of rumor. Thanks to the Greeks, we can distinguish tragedy from comedy in drama, and so we still tend to assume that each is the half of drama that is not the other half. When we come to deal with such forms as the masque, opera, movie, ballet, puppet-play, mystery-play, morality, commedia dell' arte, and Zauberspiel, we find ourselves in the position of the Renaissance doctors who refused to treat syphilis because Galen said nothing about it.[32]

* See William Skaff, *The Philosophy of T.S. Eliot: From Skepticism to a Surrealist Poetic, 1909–1927* (Philadelphia 1986).

The study of genres, Frye elsewhere explained, is based on analogies of form. Documentary and historical criticism cannot deal with such analogies. Confronted with a tragedy of Shakespeare and a tragedy of Sophocles, to be compared solely because they are both tragedies, the historical critic has to confine himself to general reflections about the seriousness of life; and the rhetorical critic only analyses what is in front of him without much regard as to whether it is a play, a lyric, or a novel. But once 'we think of a poem in relation to other poems, as a unit of poetry, we can see that the study of genres has to be founded on the study of convention. The criticism which can deal with such matters will have to be based on that aspect of symbolism which relates poems to one another, and it will choose, as its main field of operations, the symbols that link poems together.'[33]

We have three generic terms – drama, epic, and lyric – derived from the Greeks, Frye explained, but we use the latter two chiefly as jargon for long and short poems respectively. However,

the origin of the words drama, epic, and lyric suggests that the central principle of genre is simple enough. The basis of generic distinctions in literature appears to be the radical of presentation. Words may be acted in front of a listener; they may be sung or chanted; or they may be written for a reader. Criticism, we note resignedly in passing, has no word for the individual member of an author's audience, and the word 'audience' itself does not really cover all genres, as it is slightly illogical to describe the readers of a book as an audience. The basis of generic criticism in any case is rhetorical, in the sense that the genre is determined by the condition established between the poet and his public.[34]

We have to speak of 'the *radical* of presentation,' Frye added, 'if the distinctions of acted, spoken, and written word are to mean anything in the age of the printing press. One may print a lyric or read a novel aloud, but such incidental changes are not enough in themselves to alter the genre.'

McLuhan's chapter on genre opens with a statement contradictory of Frye's assertion that the critical theory of genres is precisely where Aristotle left it. 'Most of the more contemporary approaches to the theory of genres,' McLuhan contended, 'were, of course, anticipated by Shakespeare.' Indeed, it would appear that they had been anticipated by Polonius. Polonius, wrote McLuhan, 'is more circumstantial in classifying the modes in which as Professor Frye says, "words may be acted before a spectator" ...' Polonius, he further observed, 'retrieves his archetypal forms from a much larger store of traditional rhetoric than Professor Frye dips into'; at which point he quotes from *Hamlet*, Act II, Scene 2:

POLONIUS: The best actors in the world, either for tragedy, comedy, history, pastoral, pastoral-comical-historical-pastoral, tragical-historical, tragical-comical-historical-pastoral, scene individable, or poem unlimited; Seneca cannot be too heavy, nor Plautus too light. For the law of writ and liberty, these are the only men.

In tossing this collection of genres at Frye, McLuhan was perhaps being only half-way serious; but he did seriously differ with him. His serious objection to the *Anatomy of Criticism* was that: 'Working entirely from the medium of the printed word, Professor Frye has developed a classification of literary forms that ignores not only the print process as it created a special type of writer and audience, but all other media as well ...'

In the twentieth century, McLuhan contended, 'the effect of nonprint media on literature has been as extensive as it has been on psychology and anthropology, from which Professor Frye derives many of his categories of classification.'[35] Further: 'By ignoring the oral tradition of both preliterate and postliterate cultures, Professor Frye sets up a system of classifications that apply to a recent segment of human technology and culture – a segment that is rapidly dissolving. If we are restricted to Professor Frye's categories of printed literature, the entire history of genre from Homer to the present – a subject enriched by thousands of poets and scholars in explicit commentary on their works – is resignedly ignored.'[36] McLuhan devoted the rest of the chapter to enlarging Frye's concept of 'genre.' Indeed he may be said to have dragged the term through the chapter 'like a dog's coat gathering burrs,' gathering theatrical forms, legal forms – the forms of action at law – forms of song and speech and dance; indeed far more forms than can be conveniently treated here.

Frye and McLuhan also differed as to the meaning assigned to the word 'symbol,' which was defined by the former as 'Any unit of any work of literature which can be isolated for critical attention. In general usage restricted to the smaller units, such as words, phrases, images, etc.'[37] According to him, an 'archetype' was such a 'symbol.' 'The problem of convention,' Frye had observed,

is the problem of how art can be communicable, for literature is clearly as much a technique of communication as assertive verbal structures are. Poetry, taken as a whole, is no longer simply an aggregate of artifacts imitating nature, but one of the activities of human artifice taken as a whole ... [Here we are] concerned ... with the social aspect of poetry, with poetry as the focus of a community. The symbol in this phase is the communicable unit, to which I give the name archetype: that is, a typical or recurring image.[38]

'I mean by an archetype,' he added, 'a symbol which connects one poem with another and thereby helps to unify and integrate our literary experience. And as the archetype is the communicable symbol, archetypal criticism is primarily concerned with literature as a social fact and as a mode of communication.' By the study of conventions and genres, Frye was attempting to fit poems into the body of poetry as a whole.

McLuhan took fundamental issue with Frye's definition of a symbol as 'any unit of any work of literature which can be isolated for critical attention. In general usage restricted to the smaller units, such as words, phrases, images, etc.' The student, he observed, might find himself in a world of chaotic and conflicting suggestions if he attempted to use this definition as 'an exploratory probe.'

'Many people,' McLuhan contended, 'confuse single objects with symbols. It helps to note the original meaning and structure of the term "symbol" as a juxtaposition of two things. Originally, parties to a contract broke a stick and each took a half. Upon completion of the relationship, the parties juxtaposed the two sticks, creating the *symbol*. It is from *symballein*, Greek for "throwing together." '[39] Symbols, McLuhan claimed, behave like metaphors. That is to say, if a symbol be isolated from its ground it ceases to be a symbol in the same way that 'barefoot' ceases to be a metaphor if isolated from 'coffee.' From McLuhan's point of view, Frye was dealing with material less forceful than boiled spinach; although boiled spinach is in no way lacking in metaphoric force when related to a proper ground.

McLuhan's usage of the term 'symbol' corresponds more closely to that of Jung than does Frye's. Jung distinguished sharply between what he termed 'symbols' and 'signs.' A red flag, for example, waved near a highway construction site, is a mere sign, signifying 'danger'; a red flag carried by a revolutionary storming the barricades is an emotive symbol, symbolizing a complex of revolutionary ideas and values. A symbol, however, could degenerate into a sign. 'The symbol,' Jung wrote, 'is alive only so long as it is pregnant with meaning. But once its meaning has been borne out of it, once the expression is found which formulates the thing sought, expected, or divined even better than the hitherto accepted symbol, then the symbol is dead, i.e., it possesses only an historical significance.'[40] This is a cliché/archetype formulation. The symbol is being treated like live and dead metaphor. It perhaps explains why McLuhan declined to define clearly what he meant by the word 'archetype.'

It will be recalled from the discussion of Innis in earlier chapters that both his writing and thinking were informed by juxtapositions of apparently unrelated ideas; and that his work was admired by McLuhan for precisely that reason. Frye's writing, on the other hand, is characterized by its precision and its exact categories. For this reason it was criticized by McLuhan. He would have assailed Aristotle for categorizing. Categories for McLuhan were clichéd concepts that blocked original perception.

Finally, McLuhan, while seeming to accept the position of Lauriat Lane as a conventional version of the archetypal question inquired as to why the word 'archetype' should relate so exclusively to literature. Pointing to the experience of another literary critic, he observed that the same thing might be said of cliché. 'When I.A. Richards was lecturing at the University of Wisconsin, he was accidentally immersed in the very cold waters of Lake Mendota while canoeing. He was rescued in an unconscious condition still clinging to the thwart of the canoe. The student paper *The Cardinal* in a feature cartoon ran the caption: "Saved by a stock response." '[41]

VI

To inquire linearly as to the derivation of McLuhan's ideas is not the most profitable means of investigation. Undoubtedly, as he himself often testified, he acquired many ideas from Innis; but it is far more important to notice the similarities and dissimilarities of his thought from that of others than to take note of linear connectedness. It is more important, for example, to note that in some respects his thought was congruent with that of Innis and that in some other respects it was not. Innis's thinking with regard to space and time, as has been indicated, had little or no influence upon him. Modern forms of communications, he contended, were abolishing space and time. He was more concerned than Innis with the discontinuous and the simultaneous. It is especially important to keep distinctions of this sort in mind when dealing with the varying concepts of archetypes discussed above.

Even as he was influenced by Innis, McLuhan unquestionably was influenced by Carl Jung. As early as 1944, long before he had moved beyond purely literary criticism, he wrote: 'Increasingly, I feel that Catholics must master C.G. Jung. The little self-conscious (unearned) area in which we live to-day has nothing to do with the problems of our faith. Modern anthropology and psychology are more important for the Church than St. Thomas to-day.'[42] To what extent, then, do his ideas correspond with those of Jung? In answering this question one must keep in mind that Jung's concept of an archetype as a form forever buried in the collective unconscious does not fit into McLuhan's cliché/archetype pattern; for an archetype so buried could never become clichéd.

The same thing, however, cannot be said of the archetypal imagery to which Jungian archetypes give rise in consciousness. Images of this sort move from archetype to cliché and back again easily enough, as Jung himself took note. McLuhan's notion of the relationship of archetypes and clichés to the unconscious, however, corresponds not only with the analytical psychology of C.G. Jung but also with certain of the literary criticism of T.S. Eliot, most notably with Eliot's description of 'the auditory imagination.' 'What I call the "auditory imagination," ' Eliot wrote,

is the feeling for syllable and rhythm, penetrating far below the conscious levels of thought and feeling, invigorating every word; sinking to
the most primitive and forgotten, returning to the origin and bringing
something back, seeking the beginning and the end. It works through
meanings, certainly, or not without meanings in the ordinary sense,
and fuses the old and obliterated and the trite, the current, and the
new and surprising, the most ancient and the most civilized mentality.*

This passage appears as an epigraph in the chapter 'Consciousness' in *From Cliché to Archetype*. It also appears frequently in
McLuhan's other publications and in his private correspondence. It is the 'auditory imagination,' then, that penetrating
the unconscious, fuses the old, the obliterated, and the trite
with the current, the new, and the surprising. This, McLuhan
appears to have thought, pertained to the genius of the great
artist, most notably to modernist writers, to Yeats and Pound
and Eliot and Joyce, all of whom concerned themselves with the
unconscious.

McLuhan's treatment of the archetype to a large extent *corresponds* with that of Jung; and his view of the relationship of
consciousness with the unconscious *corresponds* with that of Eliot.
In a similar fashion his view of the relationship of the cliché to
the archetype *corresponds* with that of the poet William Butler
Yeats's 'The Circus Animals' Desertion,' from which McLuhan
quotes in his eccentrically located 'Introduction.'

> *I sought a theme and sought for it in vain,*
> *I sought it daily for six weeks or so.*
> *Maybe at last, being but a broken man,*

---

* As quoted in *From Cliché to Archetype*, 63. The quotation is from 'Matthew
Arnold' in T.S. Eliot's *The Use of Poetry and the Use of Criticism* (London
1933), 118–19.

> *I must be satisfied with my heart, although*
> *Winter and summer till old age began*
> *My circus animals were all on show,*
> *Those stilted boys, that burnished chariot,*
> *Lion and woman and the Lord knows what.*

Of these lines, McLuhan observed that they are a retrieval of Yeats's entire career. 'Seeing himself as an old man, he has thrown himself on the scrap heap. He has archetypalized himself, but first he rehearses all the clichés of his art, all the innovations that he had introduced into the drama and poetry of his time.' Here McLuhan pointed to the line 'What can I but enumerate old themes?' to observe that, having surveyed these stages of his art, Yeats simply says,

> *Those masterful images because complete*
> *Grew in pure mind, but out of what began?*

The answer Yeats gives to this question, McLuhan asserted, presents the main theme of *From Cliché to Archetype*. Yeats's new poetic techniques and images are retrived from

> *A mound of refuse or the sweepings of a street,*
> *Old kettles, old bottles, and a broken can,*
> *Old iron, old bones, old rags, that raving slut*
> *Who keeps the till ...*

The images retrieved from ' "the rag and bone shop", out of which he built his ladder for the high-wire act,' McLuhan explains, 'are now complete and cast aside. His "Jacob's ladder" is gone.'[43] Jacob's ladder to heaven, it would appear, was Yeats's ladder to the unconscious. And Yeats's poem provided the governing metaphor, model, or paradigm for McLuhan's carefully crafted book.

FIVE

FORMAL CAUSALITY APPLIED

I

Marshall McLuhan and, according to him, Harold Innis too were fundamentally concerned with what McLuhan termed 'formal causality.' This expression had been used by Aristotle who, drawing upon the precedents of even earlier thinkers, distinguished among four different kinds of causes or explanatory principles. 'These,' writes Richard Taylor,

he called the 'efficient' cause (*causa quod*), or that by which some change is wrought; the 'final' cause (*causa ut*), or end or purpose for which a change is produced; the 'material' cause, or that in which a change is wrought; and the 'formal' cause, or that into which some thing is changed. Thus, for example, a statue is produced by a sculptor (its efficient cause) by his imposing changes upon a piece of marble (its material cause) for the purpose of possessing a beautiful object (its final cause), the marble thereby acquiring the form, or distinctive properties, of a statue (its formal cause).[1]

The concepts of material and formal causes, Taylor added, 'are archaic and now have little significance outside aesthetics.'

By 'formal causality,' however, McLuhan meant something rather different than did Aristotle and Taylor. He referred to formal cause, he once explained, not in the sense of classification of forms, but of their operation upon us and upon one another.[2] This was what he meant when he treated figure/ground relationships. It was also what he meant by 'the medium is the message,' that it was the form of the medium, generally unnoticed or ignored, rather than its content, that was significant. Innis, according to McLuhan, was the first modern scholar to employ formal causality. 'As soon as the reader grasps that Innis is concerned with the unique power of each form to alter the action of other forms it encounters, he will be able to proceed as Innis did.'[3] McLuhan himself was to do just that.

Although he never referred to it as formal causality, it was in this way that Harold Innis distinguished between the communications system of the St Lawrence and its shifting staple content. The rivalry of this communications system with those of the Hudson River and Hudson Bay, Innis indicated, had formative influences upon Canada. It is this that unites his early work with what came later. It likewise unites McLuhan's early media studies with his application of the grammar of language to other technologies in works like *From Cliché to Archetype*. A search for, and study of, 'formal' causes, in this sense of the word, lies at the very heart of the work of both Innis and McLuhan.

Their methodology can have fruitful applications. In this chapter it will be applied to the history of Canada, specifically to two clichéd forms, or artifacts, of Canadian political discourse that in the nineteenth and early twentieth centuries entered into fundamental historical explanation. One of these artifacts, the phrase 'family compact,' was once a metaphor; the other, the term 'responsible government,' began life as a political slogan and ended as a concept of political science. Both were closely related; and both were keystones in the structure of a Canadian version of 'the Whig interpretation of history.' It was against this clichéd interpretation that Donald Creighton wrote in reaction in and after the 1930s; but it was a historical explanation from which he himself never entirely escaped. It was this same tradition from which Harold Innis broke completely. Thus we are examining the 'ground' from which, in quite different ways, the work of both Creighton and Innis emerged as 'figures.'

II

The concepts of causality that inform most if not all Whig interpretations are those that Aristotle termed 'efficient' and, to a lesser degree, 'final.' Whig interpretations are stories of struggles engaged in by men (the efficient cause) for liberty (the final cause). Notably absent from these explanations is any sense of what Aristotle, to say nothing of McLuhan, understood to be formal causality.

The particular struggle for liberty that concerns us here is one alleged to have taken place in certain of the colonies of British North America between the years 1791 and 1848, the final implications of which were thought to have worked themselves out only in 1931, the year that saw passage of the Statute of Westminster. This act conceded Canada almost complete autonomy within the British Commonwealth of Nations.* These struggles were perceived as having been fought out between reform politicians in locally elected assemblies and constitutionally entrenched oligarchies, the cliché/archetype of which was the family compact of Upper Canada.

One of the more significant and interesting aspects of this archetype is that historians, and before them politicians, could never agree upon what it actually was. In 1915, for example, W.S. Wallace wrote of it as 'a local oligarchy composed of men, some well-born, some ill-born, some brilliant, some stupid, whom the caprices of a small provincial society ... had pitchforked into power.'[4] Then in 1926 Alison Ewart and Julia Jarvis identified this compact exclusively with the personnel of the Upper Canadian executive and legislative councils that sat between 1791 and 1841.[5] Only one year later, however, Aileen Dunham contended that it stood for 'a tendency of society rather than for a definite organization.'[6]

In the next decade Donald Creighton conceived of it as not having been confined to the colony of Upper Canada. The Family Compact 'in both Upper and Lower Canada,' he wrote, 'was less a company of blood-relations than it was a fraternal

---

* Power to amend the British North America Act remained with the parliament at Westminster, and the Judicial Committee of the Privy Council remained a final court of appeal.

union of merchants, professional men and bureaucrats. The group was relatively small; and the names of a few dozen persons turn up again and again, with almost equal regularity in the affairs of business and of government, until the extent of their monopoly control suggests the practical identification of the political and commercial state.'[7] In 1952, however, Hugh Aitken, while viewing business interests as interwoven with the compact, nonetheless regarded it as distinct from them.[8] Then, apparently influenced by C. Wright Mills,* R.E. Saunders in 1957 treated the family compact as a sort of 'power élite.'[9] And sociological concepts of élite groups have since then influenced the thinking of S.F. Wise, a leading authority upon conservative traditions in Upper Canada.[10]

Of recent studies, the most significant are those of Wise and the late G.M. Craig, whose *Upper Canada: The Formative Years* is the best and most recent book-length history of the colony. The epithet 'family compact,' wrote Craig in 1963, 'had only a limited accuracy since, as Lord Durham later pointed out, its members were not all tied together by family connection, nor were they the ingrown, selfish, and reactionary group that the phrase was meant by their opponents to suggest.' Yet he thought the term continued 'to be useful to describe the relatively small, tightly knit group of men who dominated the government of Upper Canada in the 1820's and to a somewhat lesser extent in the following decade.'[11] But he did not explain why the term continued to be useful nor did he explain why he departed from Durham's concept by limiting the group's membership to 'simply the leading members of the administration: executive councillors, senior officials, and certain members of the judiciary.' In this latter regard S.F. Wise the previous year had followed Durham more nearly by equating the compact not with a small

* C. Wright Mills, *The Power Elite* (New York 1956).

group of officials but with a whole social class. 'It was virtually identical (with some notable exceptions),' he wrote, 'with the small professional, clerical, and mercantile middle and upper middle class ... and could claim, with a good deal of justification, a virtual monopoly of what education and general cultivation there existed in the colony.'[12]

Then, in 1967, Wise thought about the compact in a new way. 'Our reform tradition,' he wrote, 'has telescoped the complexities of early conservatism into High Toryism and turned the phrase "Family Compact" into a term of political science when it was nothing but a political epithet.'[13] Wise was on the right track; but the term 'family compact' was, and is, much more than a political epithet.

Like the St Lawrence River, it is a form that has had much shifting content. It is a *label* that, over many years, has been attached to a great many differing, often mutually contradictory ideas, only some of which may be regarded as concepts of political science. It has also been evocative of very strong political passions. Sometimes the term has meant faction united by kinship; at other times it has denoted a combination of groups united only by common interest. It has often referred to oligarchy, to quasi-aristocracy, to the administrative personnel of government, or to some combination of these and other elements. Indeed, 'the family compact' has often been treated as being synonymous with 'the Tory party,' or equated with that party's leadership.

Almost all modern writers have thought of the term as referring to some sort of group. Aileen Dunham, it is true, once referred to it as 'a tendency in society'; but this did not prevent her from elsewhere thinking of it as a company of persons. But among all writers there has been no agreement as to the nature of the entity in question, as to whether it emerged with the Constitutional Act in 1791 or took on form only in the 1820s;

as to whether it was a small group or a very large one. And, more often than not, the term has been used so ambiguously as to be evocative of several, if not many, possible meanings.

The term has thus functioned as a symbol. At one level it fits Northrop Frye's definition of a symbol, namely: 'Any unit of any work of literature which can be isolated for critical attention. In general usage restricted to the smaller units, such as words, phrases, images, etc.' But beyond this it was a highly affective symbol that was much more than a mere sign. It may also be usefully studied as a cliché/archetype.

The term has never been studied as a symbol. With the exception of S.F. Wise in 1967, all historians have assumed that 'the family compact' had some sort of existence outside the realm of pure ideas that was discernible and definable. This emphasis upon *literal* meaning has had very important consequences. On the one hand it has left the label, stripped of meanings inappropriate to particular contexts, structurally intact as a governing component of historical thought. Thus it remained integrated in the thought of a Creighton, a Craig, or a Wise – none of whom agreed with another as to its meaning – even as long ago it had been part of the conceptual apparatus of the radical Upper Canadian journalist William Lyon Mackenzie. On the other hand, this same insistence upon literal meaning has blocked appreciation of the fact that the term quite properly had diverse, contradictory meanings, and that this has been essential to its function as a symbol. Its symbolic force, moreover, did not arise from sets of ideas that can be characterized simply as concepts of political science. Symbolic force arose from highly affective ideas emotively related to particular historical and ideological contexts, and from the relationship of these ideas to opposing clusters of concepts subsumed by the expression 'responsible government.' These unexamined relationships, however, have largely been stripped away by twentieth-century historical revision.

Like 'family compact,' 'responsible government' is a term that, over the course of time, has denoted a variety of differing concepts. In contrast to the former expression, however, its meaning is today more or less fixed, scholars being in agreement that it signifies cabinet responsibility to a popularly elected chamber in a modern form of parliamentary democracy. But such has not always been the case. In the late nineteenth century it also meant self-government; and in an earlier period it simply meant the opposite of tyrannical government.

The term was coined in the early 1830s, most probably by the radical William Lyon Mackenzie, who set it in opposition to what he understood by compact rule. At a literal level it then referred to certain constitutional ideas that had been entertained earlier by Baldwinite reformers and the Thorpe Party in Upper Canada, by leaders of the Parti Canadien in Lower Canada, and by eighteenth-century politicians who had struggled in Ireland to secure the independence of the parliament at Dublin from that at Westminster.

By the twentieth century these facts had been forgotten or were in the process of being ignored. Constitutional historians – of whom Aileen Dunham and Chester Martin will serve as examples here – distinguished between the term 'responsible government' and what it denoted only to establish what they took to be its *correct* meaning. These writers, moreover, entertained most misleading evolutionary presuppositions about the nature of constitutional development and treated responsible government as though it were a single concept. Dunham, for example, believed that 'the idea of responsible government' had first been conceived of about 1828 by the reform politician William Warren Baldwin who even then, in terms of constitutional development in Great Britain, was in advance of his times. She, Martin, and many others, believed that the idea had been transmitted by Baldwin and his son Robert to Lord Durham in 1838, and that it had been duly implemented during the administration of Lord Elgin a decade later. The school to which these writers belonged has been criticized by Creighton and others for its dull, dry-as-dust approach to history; but its essential soundness has never been challenged. Much scholarly confusion has ensued, of which only a few representative examples can be considered here.

In 1965 K.W. Windsor published the first modern survey of the writings of nineteenth-century historians of Canada. 'It is astonishing,' he then observed, 'that most of these historians did not seem to know when responsible government actually came into existence.'[14] William Kingsford, he noted, thought it was established with the act of union in 1841; and he remarked with surprise that in 1907 Stephen Leacock had found it necessary to point out that 'the interpretation of the principle of responsible government now prevailing was not present in the minds of imperial statesmen at the time of the adoption of the Act of Union of 1840, commonly assigned as the date of the inception of self-government.' The implications of Leacock's remark, however, did not dawn on Windsor. With what had become the orthodox view firmly in mind, he could not see that Kingsford and others were not grossly mistaken, that by 'responsible government' they merely understood something other than did he, that since they had written the term's meaning had shifted. In point of fact it was reasonable for these early historians to write as they did; for in 1840 the constitutional structures thought to have sustained compact government were overthrown, and what was then understood by 'responsible government' was entirely achieved.

Whether the theory associated with the term 'responsible government' emerged from political struggles within the colonies or was borrowed from the political practice of the United Kingdom is a problem, related to the meaning of words, that has confounded many writers. Dunham, for example, could never separate early demands for local ministerial responsibility

from meanings that became attached to 'responsible government' during and long after the 1840s. In the first decade of the
nineteenth century, she contended, Lower Canadian politicians
had grasped the importance of impeachment but could not
develop the theory of responsible government because it was 'a
product of the party system, and depends upon a rotation of
parties in power.'[15] While this reasoning was entirely inconsis-
tent with her conviction that Baldwin had formulated just such
a theory long before parties rotated in power in Upper Canada,
her main point was that divisions in the Lower Canadian assembly were of race, not of party, 'that the French [Canadians] were
a permanent majority, and power could not shift back and forth
between them and the English [Canadians].' But beyond this
she could not believe that ministerial responsibility, which to
her was synonymous with responsible government, could have
been understood in this early period. The theory, to be sure,
had been grasped in Upper Canada, but this could not have
been long before it had been practised in Britain, which could
not have been much before the passage of the Reform Act of
1832. Colonials, she reasoned, were unlikely to have been more
'clear-sighted than the mother country.'

This historian's confusion of mind continues to perplex the
history of Lower Canada. Unknown to or forgotten by Dunham,
Governor Craig reported in 1808 that the Parti Canadien,
'either believe, or affect to believe that there exists a Ministry
here, and that in imitation of the Constitution of Great Britain
that Ministry is responsible to them for the conduct of Government.'[16] Now, while this went well beyond anything Dunham
had believed possible, it would be a mistake to call it responsible
government, a label that had yet to be invented. For to do so is to
risk confounding early ideas with others that became associated
with the term much later, and further confounding ideas developed in Britain with others that emerged in the colonies.

This happened in 1972 when Fernand Ouellet, without making the above distinction, challenged some of Dunham's theories to conclude that, in the first decade of the nineteenth century, Canadian politicians 'commencèrent à parler de gouvernement responsable.'[17] Aileen Dunham's argument, Ouellet contended, 'exagère en plus la dépendance intellectuelle des coloniaux à l'égard des cerveaux de la mère-patrie. Il n'est absolument pas évident que les colons ... avaient besoin des métropolitains pour découvrir le gouvernement responsable.' Persuaded that the theory of responsible government 'était moins le résultat d'un exercice intellectual qu'un élément fondamental dans la stratégie du nouveau parti auquel ils appartenaient,' he concluded that both political parties 'et l'idée de responsabilité ministérielle furent après 1800 le produit d'une société [canadienne] agitée et en transition.'[18]

Thus he fell back upon a set of ideas reminiscent of those of Chester Martin who had argued that the theory of responsible government emerged from party conflicts within the colonial legislatures of the Second British Empire.[19] But unless one is prepared to believe that persons like Governor Craig acquired their understanding of what Ouellet terms 'gouvernement responsable' from spokesmen of the Parti Canadien, theses of this sort are untenable. The truth of the matter is that both Craig and the Lower Canadians acquired their understanding of ministerial responsibility from the same source: les cerveaux de la mère-patrie.*

III

Thus, while there has been little twentieth-century agreement as to the meaning of 'family compact,' agreement upon the

---

* For the strong influence of English ideas upon the minds of the Parti Canadien see L.A.H. Smith, 'Le Canadien and the British Constitution,

meaning of 'responsible government' has only served to grab the mind and cripple the understanding. But to understand how this interesting and highly significant phenomenon was produced, one must examine how these two forms functioned in relation to each other in the nineteenth century.

Of the two terms, 'family compact' is the older. It was almost unknown, however, during the 1820s – the period in which the several entities it later denoted are commonly supposed to have flourished – and it remained almost unknown until it was popularized in the 1830s by W.L. Mackenzie. When he did this, moreover, the term's meaning was radically changed. Hence most of the concepts later attached to the form are anachronisms when projected into earlier periods.

Of these anachronisms the most immediately significant is the conviction that a family compact was some sort of group. In the beginning the word 'compact' did not refer to a clique, faction, party, oligarchy, or collectivity of persons of any sort. It meant understanding, agreement, or treaty. Initially it was simply the English translation of *Pacte de Famille*, the name given to first a single treaty, that of 1733 between the French and Spanish branches of the House of Bourbon, and later to a series of treaties within the same dynasty that also embraced the Kingdom of the Two Sicilies. The eighteenth-century use of the term is well revealed by the response a Spanish secretary of state once made to a British protest against the extension of this compact to embrace the House of Habsburg. 'Nothing could embarrass us so much,' declared the Marchese Grimaldi, 'as the court of Vienna's desire to accede to the Family Compact.' For it, he continued, 'is an *affaire de coeur* and not an *affaire politique*. The moment any other Power that is not of the family accedes to it,

---

1806–1810,' *Canadian Historical Review* (1957); Helen Taft Manning, *The Revolt of French Canada* (Toronto 1962), ch. 4.

it becomes a political affair, and may alarm Europe, which is the furthest from our thoughts.'[20]

The French word '*pacte*' cannot possibly refer to a group of people; and initially neither could the English word 'compact.' As is indicated later this change of meaning took place some time in the mid- or late 1820s in Upper Canada. Meanwhile, it would experience significant shifts of meaning elsewhere.

At the end of the eighteenth century, the form crossed the Atlantic to enter the rhetoric of Barnabas Bidwell. He was a doctrinaire Jeffersonian pamphleteer resident in Massachusetts at a time of bitter political warfare between his party and the Federalists.

Political parties in the United States were then just emerging; and Bidwell was an important organizer of the Democratic-Republicans and of the Jeffersonian partisan press.* He employed the term 'family compact' metaphorically in a pejorative fashion against Theodore Sedgewick, a local Federalist notable. Sedgewick, it appeared, was possessed of 'the influence of numerous connections formed into a phalanx by family compact.'[21] Significantly, it is 'phalanx' and not 'compact' that here denotes faction; 'compact' still refers only to a form of covenant. And Bidwell, it is clear, well understood the expression's original meaning. The natural condition of European countries, he once argued elsewhere, was to be at war with their neighbours, contiguous countries being natural rivals. That this condition did not always obtain, however, he accounted for by 'family compacts and other intervening causes.'[22]

Thus, at a literal level, the term still denoted much of what it had in the past. But employed in a new American context the form acquired new connotations. For in Bidwell's mind, and in many minds of the republican public he sought to persuade,

---

* I have treated Bidwell at length in the *Dictionary of Canadian Biography*, vol. 6, 54–8.

family compacts were associated with monarchies, of which they tended not to think well. Monarchy was associated with British tradition, from which they had recently violently broken, and which Bidwell, for one, held to be alien to American tradition. The former tradition he associated with the political objectives of his Federalist enemies; and these he held to be nefarious. Thus, in this new context of American party warfare, the term became a highly charged political and national symbol.

As a man of very considerable ability, Bidwell prospered. He became the leading spokesman in the House of Representatives for President Jefferson; and in 1810 he was being considered for appointment to the Supreme Court of the United States by President Madison. Then he was overtaken by disaster. Bidwell was treasurer of the county of Berkshire in Massachusetts. In 1810 discrepancies were found in his accounts. Fearing prosecution, he then fled to Upper Canada, carrying with him the clichéd forms of his eighteenth-century republican rhetoric.

Those rhetorical forms thereby found a new context. George III's colony of Upper Canada had been settled initially in the late 1780s by refugees from the American War of Independence who called themselves 'United Empire Loyalists.' By 1810, however, this group was greatly outnumbered by more recent settlers from the United States pejoratively referred to by the refugees as 'late loyalists.' This term implied that these settlers were not really loyal at all, that they had come to the colony merely for the sake of the free land to which loyalists were entitled. When political opposition opened between these two groups, so too opened a rhetoric of loyalty, on the one hand, and a rhetoric of republicanism, on the other. The latter sort of rhetoric in some instances stemmed from prior ideological commitment; but in many other cases opposition to the established institutions of Upper Canada gave birth to republican commitment. The language of republicanism, after all, was the only language of opposition with which most of these people were at all familiar. But whatever the case, when understood within the context of the then very strained British-American relations, and against the very real threat of invasion by American armies, this rhetoric gave rise to intense concern on the part of those who supported the established government. Thus when Bidwell, who settled near the town of Kingston, became involved in these controversies, he became an object of suspicion. And, by reason of his acknowledged political and intellectual ability, he became much feared.

In 1821 he unsuccessfully stood for election to the House of Assembly. In the following year, however, the elected candidate died; and Bidwell was returned in an ensuing by-election. The House of Assembly then resolved that he was ineligible to take his seat; and this gave rise to the 'Alien Issue,' which tore at the body politic of the province until 1828.

It is against this background, and out of the town of Kingston where Bidwell was politically active, that a derivative of the clichéd form 'family compact' first surfaces in print. As S.F. Wise has noticed, the term 'all one family compacted junto' appears in a pamphlet published at Kingston in 1824 by Thomas Dalton. 'It rather looks,' Wise wrote, 'as if Thomas Dalton ought to be given the credit, long awarded to [W.L.] Mackenzie, of first applying the term "family compact" to a section of the Upper Canadian ruling group.'[23]

There are a number of points to be noticed here. First, Dalton, in point of fact, did not employ the exact phrase 'family compact.' The expression he did use – 'all one family compacted junto' – differs from Mackenzie's usage in that 'junto', not 'compact' refers to the collectivity in question. It also differs from Bidwell's usage in that 'compacted' is not a noun meaning *agreement* but an adjective meaning *agreed*, but possibly also meaning *compressed*. Second, the epithet was directed at what Wise, but not Dalton, conceived of as 'a section of the Upper Canadian ruling group.' In this particular context the latter was solely concerned with a clique of Kingstonians. This is an important point because, while the Kingston group could more or less plausibly be thought of as being united by marriage or kinship, the much larger provincial group certainly could not be.

Dalton, in contrast to Bidwell, was not a republican. A hot-tempered brewer and sometime bank director, he shortly became one of the colony's most outspoken Tory editors. His ire in this instance, however, was directed at a group of four men: Christopher Hagerman, who represented Kingston in the House of Assembly; and three others, John Macaulay, John Kirby, and George Markland, all of whom had been appointed through the influence of Hagerman to investigate a bank failure in which Dalton had been involved. But by 1824 these men were also long-standing political enemies of Bidwell; and all, with the exception of Markland, were related by marriage to Hagerman or each other.

The chances are that Dalton simply borrowed an expression previously used by Bidwell to describe the local group to which these men belonged. The form and content of the cliché have been slightly modified; but the important point is that neither Bidwell nor Dalton was at all likely to have used either form to stigmatize any group that did not appear to be united by family ties.

The Bidwellian origins of the expression are further indicated by the fact that the earliest Canadian record of the *exact* phrase is to be discovered in the private correspondence of Barnabas's son, Marshall, who was elected in his father's place to the House of Assembly. 'I shall be happy to consult with you and Mr. [John] Rolph,' young Bidwell wrote to William Baldwin in 1828, 'on measures to relieve this province of the evils which a family compact have [*sic*] brought upon it.'[24] The content and context of Bidwell's letter leave the meaning of 'family compact' quite unclear. His use of the plural form 'have' following the singular noun 'compact' might suggest that he was referring to a collectivity of persons. On the other hand it may merely be a grammatical error. It would be rash to assume that he had radically departed from the usage of his father with which he must have been quite familiar.

Yet, although the evidence is scant and inconclusive, the phrase was then perhaps already in the process of acquiring something like its later meanings. Five years previously, in 1823, Charles Fothergill, editor of the York *Weekly Register*, had written of a 'vast innoxious [*sic*] vapour,' which had 'issued from the COMPACT through the [York] *Observer* last week.'[25] No reference was made to the idea of family; and the exact political context of the remark has been lost. But, within the context of the remark itself, the word 'compact' would seem to make more sense if it referred to a cabal of some sort, rather than to the understanding uniting it. It is perhaps significant that when the word 'compact' re-emerges with the former meaning it is again from York, this time through the agency of Mackenzie.

By 1823 both Bidwells had been active at York defending themselves against petitioners from their riding of Lennox and Addington who, headed by their old Kingston enemies, were attempting to unseat them from the assembly. It is possible that one or both of them made references that were imperfectly understood at York to a family compact uniting this Kingston clan, and that it was there the phrase began to take on new meaning.

Be this as it may, it is significant that during this period the expression was not used by the Bidwells' own party organ, the *Upper Canada Herald* of Kingston. The reason is obvious. In this period the main objects of the *Herald*'s polemic were the advisers of Lieutenant-Governor Maitland in the Executive Council and their supporters in the Legislative Council and the House of Assembly. This group was clearly not united by marriage; and, as yet, it had occurred to no one to suggest otherwise. The polemic that issued from the *Herald* in these years, however, did affect much later thinking about compacts, and account must be taken of it here.

During the 1820s the *Herald* was owned and edited by Hugh Thomson. A non-republican radical, he was then allied with the Bidwells. But in contrast to the radicalism of the Bidwells, or to that of Mackenzie in the 1830s, his radicalism seems to have been informed by a clichéd set of ideas embedded in Whig interpretations of British history, notably by a set of ideas first propagated by Lord Bolingbroke in the eighteenth century. Thus the main object of his attacks was not a family compact united by kinship, but a court party united by selfish interest.

In histories read by Thomson and others of his generation a 'Country Party,' broadly representative of the interests of Britain as a whole but out of power, was conceived of as existing in opposition to a narrowly based, self-interested 'Court Party,' which was in power. By upsetting the delicate balance of the English constitution this latter body was held to have threatened the country with a form of despotism.* A mirror image of this cliché is to be found reflected in the pages of Thomson's *Herald*.

In 1825 the *Kingston Chronicle*, an organ of the executive, charged the radicals in the assembly with unpatriotic, partisan obstruction for opposing passage of a supply bill. In a series of pseudonymous letters alleged to have been written to the editor, but that more probably were a series of editorials written by the editor himself, the *Herald* launched a counter-attack upon what was termed a 'court party.'

This body was said to be headed by the Archdeacon of York, John Strachan, one of the principal advisers of the lieutenant-governor, Sir Peregrine Maitland. 'Everybody knows,' wrote

---

* See, for example, Henry St John Bolingbroke's *A Dissertation upon Parties, in Several Letters to Caleb D'Anvers Esq.* (London 1735) and David Hume's *The History of England*, vol. 6 (London, 1823), note k 560–4, also vol. 8, 126.

one 'Hampden,' 'that the little bigot of little York [Strachan] and his pupils, parasites and sycophants ... dislike the present house, but the people will not upon their account think their representatives unfaithful servants.'[26] That the assembly should tamely pass supplies requested by a governor advised by interested parties, he continued, was the 'court party's' favourite political doctrine, a doctrine 'subversive of the vital principle of our constitution.' In practice, it would 'convert the government into a despotism, and give the will of the Executive the practical force and effect of law.' And, in like fashion, the *Herald* was darkly suspicious of the motives of Kingston's representative, Christopher Hagerman, who, apparently in an effort to give a more 'respectable' tone to the deliberations of his tumultuous chamber, had proposed abolishing the members' pay. This step, it appeared, was calculated to make representatives of moderate income dependent upon executive patronage. 'Such a state of Court influence, the most subtle species of bribery, would tend to render members really representative of the Crown, instead of, as the Constitution intends, the Representatives of the People.'[27]

Theory of this sort derived from eighteenth-century concepts of a balanced constitution. In crucial respects it was contradictory of later nineteenth-century notions of responsible government that superseded it. For in the latter, the executive did not 'balance' the elected chamber but was 'responsible' to it.

Court party theory clearly owed at least as much to the English literary background and historical understanding of the writer as it did to any direct observation of political actuality in Upper Canada. Directly or indirectly it derived from Henry St John Bolingbroke's *A Dissertation upon Parties* of 1735 and from writers like David Hume, whose contemporary *History of England* was published in 1823.

It is a literary experience of a different but similar sort that connects the early Upper Canadian notion of a court party with later concepts of family compacts. In this case it is a literary experience that proceeded from a reading of the columns of the *Herald*; and of other newspapers influenced by it, for compact theory of the 1830s owed much to the clichéd court party rhetoric of the 1820s.

Both family compacts and court parties were said to have pursued the same sort of self-interested politics, and to have sought to impose a despotic will upon free-born British subjects. The idea of a court party, however, differed significantly from most notions of compacts. The composition of the entities in question of course differed; but, beyond this, so too did related, underlying constitutional theory. For while court parties were conceived of as juntos that had corruptly seized control of a very sound system of government, compacts tended to be thought of as part of the system of government, and, indeed, to have been built into the social and economic structures of the province. Hence compacts tended to be revolutionary in their implications as court parties were not. These latter *figures* were the products of the changed, radicalized political *ground* of the 1830s.

By 1833 certain ideas associated with the evolved and fundamentally altered notion of a *pacte de famille* became related in the mind of W.L. Mackenzie with others that had been associated with the Upper Canadian court party. He then produced the first construct of a family compact as a collectivity of persons of which we have extensive record.[28] According to him this was a phalanx* of about thirty persons, whose family ties he exposed in detail. Indeed, the very small size of the group was the logical consequence of the overriding importance he assigned to family ties. Thus Mackenzie included only half the six members of

* The same word 'phalanx,' it will be recalled, had been used by Barnabas Bidwell in 1800 to refer to the group that surrounded the Federalist Theodore Sedgewick of Massachusetts.

the executive council, while of the thirty-two members of the legislative council, he included only the speaker and eight others. Family connections, however, enabled him to include three chief justices, of whom one was the aforesaid speaker, and two Crown lawyers who, unfortunately for his immediate purpose, had just been dismissed from office. Beyond these officials, he included the president, solicitor, half the directors, and an unspecified number of shareholders of the Bank of Upper Canada, as well as an equally unspecified number of persons said to control the Canada Company.

This compact of Mackenzie, it should be remarked, exercised power very much after the fashion of a court party. It surrounded the governor, whom it moulded like wax; and it filled offices with its partisans. The whole of the provincial revenues were at its members' mercy; 'they are the paymasters, receivers, auditors, King, Lords and Commons.'[29]

It is a mutated version of this Mackenzie concept – stripped of all notion of family connection and expanded to embrace the Tory party – that informs Lord Durham's *Report* of 1839. According to Durham, 'family compact' was 'a name not much more appropriate than party designations usually are, inasmuch as there is, in truth, very little of family connexion among the persons thus united.'[30] It had, however, entrenched itself in the political and economic structures of the province by means of control over the executive and legislative councils. The party's bulk, the *Report* continued, consisted of native-born inhabitants and of emigrants who had settled prior to the War of 1812. 'The bench, the high offices of the episcopal church and a great deal of the legal profession are filled by adherents of this party; by grant or purchase they acquired nearly the whole of the waste lands of the Province, they are all powerful in the chartered banks and, till lately, shared among themselves almost exclusively all offices of trust and profit.'

Durham's concept was in turn transformed when it was

abstracted from its particular Upper Canadian context. Durham's disgraced predecessor in the colony, Sir Francis Bond Head, did this when he noticed that native-born inhabitants, the bench, the magistracy, and other elements alluded to by Durham formed a family compact just as much in England as in Canada, and just as much in Germany as in England. This perception proceeded, of course, from a very conservative point of view; for, to Head's way of thinking, Durham was assailing the normal structures of civilized societies. But radicals of the left were quick to make the same sort of observation.

'The FAMILY COMPACT of U.[pper] C.[anada],' wrote one such radical Irish immigrant, '... is well described by Matthew Carey in his IRELAND VINDICATED. He says: "in every subjugated country there is always a small body of natives, who make a regular contract, not written but well understood, and duly carried into effect, by which they sell the nation to its oppressors, and themselves as slaves, for the sorry pleasure of tyrannizing over their fellow slaves." '[31] The expression 'family compact,' of course, had not been used by Carey;* but Durham's usage had found a new frame of reference in this Irish reader's mind. 'These wretches,' he observed of the leaders of the Canadian compact, 'are to Upper Canada what the leaders of "the Protestant Ascendancy" have been to Ireland, a perpetual blight, the evil principle personified.' The cliché was taking on new vigour.

In a like manner, the Council of Twelve of Nova Scotia was to be identified with a family compact of sorts by other readers and writers, as was the Château Clique of Lower Canada. Indeed, a 'family company compact' would eventually be discovered in the far west. Thus the context within which Durham had placed his remarks shifted. And, with this shift, the meaning of 'family compact' also shifted.

* The reference is to Matthew Carey, *Vindiciae Hibernicae: Or Ireland Vindicated* (Philadelphia 1819).

This gathering, discarding, and obscuring of diverse, overlapping literal meanings was one of the form's most significant functions; for it created political and historical illusion. It suggested that different persons, thinking about quite different things, had essentially the same thing in mind. And, when projected into the past, the term was generally so burdened with anachronism as to create a quite specious sense of historical continuity. It thereby functioned to create the notion of a *linear* historical development entertained by historians like Aileen Dunham and Chester Martin.

But, underlying the differences of *literal* meaning, there was a very real continuity of *symbolic* meaning, in the Jungian sense of the word 'symbol.' Whether used to refer to a political covenant in eighteenth-century Massachusetts or nineteenth-century Kingston, or to an oligarchy, faction, or party at some later stage of British North American history, or to the Protestant Ascendancy of Ireland, it invariably implied a detestable state of affairs felt to be intolerable. Connotations arising from these pejorative usages gave the term symbolic force of a strongly negative character. Thus strong positive value would be assigned to whatever sets of ideas were thereafter placed in opposition to notions of compact government. This was one of the leading reasons why during and long after the 1830s so much political and historical thought was polarized around 'responsible government' and its own several opposites.

IV

The demand for executive accountability to local legislatures after the changing model of cabinet responsibility to the parliament at Westminster, we have observed, is much older than has often been supposed. Demanded partly as a right of British subjects rooted in common law, and partly as a solution to local political difficulties, it was originally only part of a larger insistence upon an inalienable right of colonials to full parliamentary government. Lord Durham was to distinguish between local affairs and those of imperial concern to recommend local executive responsibility only with regard to the former. But distinctions of this sort were not attempted before the 1830s. Thus the logical end of the early demands made by Baldwin, Thorpe, Bédard, and the rest was complete self-government. Yet, at least with regard to Baldwin and Thorpe, they paradoxically insisted that their chief object was the maintenance of 'British Connection.'

Clearly the bond they had in mind was not *political*. It would seem rather to have been *cultural*. From the 1820s on, a main thrust of Baldwinite politics was that the cultural orientation of the colony should remain British, that local forms of law and government should not be Americanized.

In many ways this outlook greatly resembles that of the eighteenth-century Anglo-Irish Volunteers who struggled for the political independence of their parliament at Dublin. In Ireland William Warren Baldwin's father, Robert, who had edited the Cork *Volunteer Journal*, had been a supporter of the Volunteers. These Irish concerns, however, were of very small moment to the Scottish-born W.L. Mackenzie, who was preoccupied with grievances and injustice. Hence this cultural concern tended to be lost sight of once he labelled the Baldwin program 'responsible government.'

When the phrase, 'responsible government' replaced 'ministerial responsibility,' moreover, a plethora of confusion arose. For the former term was ambiguous as the latter was not; the concept of responsibility *to* being no longer easily distinguishable from that of responsibility *for*. Beyond this, 'responsible government' admitted a number of opposites, which 'ministerial responsibility' did not. Among these were 'unresponsible government,' 'non-responsible government,' 'irresponsible government,' and 'anti-responsible government.' Thus the term became a sort of ideological nucleus around which revolved a whole constellation of opposing ideas.

So long as these opposing ideas were all identified in the public mind with the rule of the family compact, this was of no great moment. But when Durham recommended a continuing political role for the imperial government, and when 'responsible government' became understood within this context, the fact that it had once implied autonomy – or political separation from the mother country – became obscured.

In 1836 the reformers had been routed from the assembly when Lieutenant-Governor Head fought a general election assailing the separatist implications of the demand for responsible government; and their fortunes had ebbed further with the 1837 failure of Mackenzie's rebellion, which was identified with the same separatist impulse. But with publication of Durham's *Report* in 1839 they began to recover. 'Durham meetings' were convened by the Baldwinites, where the report's recommendations were identified with their old reform program; and Francis Hincks founded the first Baldwinite organ, the Toronto *Examiner*, with the slogan 'Responsible Government' proudly fixed to its masthead. Thus Durham's recommendations, the demands of the Baldwinite reformers, and Mackenzie's old slogan slowly came to be identified in the public mind.

Durham's recommendations with respect to ministerial responsibility, however, differed from the early demands of the reformers in that they proceeded from the political situation he wished to remedy rather than from abstract legal and constitutional argument. Indeed, his reservation of legislative power to the imperial parliament was quite at odds with arguments reformers had earlier educed from law. But what is of chief interest here is the identification of his recommendation for limited local ministerial responsibility with 'responsible government.' Durham himself made no such equation. And when he used the expression 'responsible government' – which was not often – he did so in a sense entirely different from what the reformers later made standard. In referring to citizens of the United States, for example, he remarked that they lived under 'a perfectly free and eminently responsible government.'

To Durham, then, and to most of his contemporaries, the term had no specific reference to purely parliamentary forms of government. It simply meant the opposite of arbitrary government. Therefore, when the family compact seemed to have been dislodged from power, and when the executive council was transformed into a cabinet with members holding seats in the elected assembly, as was the case after 1840, it was only reasonable to conclude that responsible government had been achieved.

How then did it ever come to imply a form of government that prevailed only after 1848? It might be supposed that this was a *direct* result of the politics of the 1840s. After all, as every Canadian child was once supposed to know, 'the struggle for responsible government' did not abate but was intensified within the newly formed Province of Canada, the Baldwinite reformers of Canada West being now joined in endeavour by Louis Hippolyte Lafontaine's bloc of francophone reformers from Canada East. Of necessity the meaning of 'responsible government' again had to change. Its main opposite could no longer be 'compact government,' which had disappeared, but had to become the 'irresponsible' rule of a series of governors or of the Colonial Office in London. And of the expression's several possible meanings, emphasis now had to fall upon 'self-government.' For nearly a decade the province was flooded with a related rhetoric of responsible government; and this, one might suppose, would have had some lasting impact upon the public mind. Yet, as we have seen, it had no such impact upon the minds of early historians.

Let us take, for example, J.M. McMullen, the author of what has been called 'the standard guide to Canadian history in the second half of the nineteenth century.'[32] Like so many others, he simply fitted what he knew of the Canadian political experience to a clichéd pattern of history that pre-existed in his mind. In this instance it was, of course, English 'Whig' history.

In England, according to McMullen, responsible government had been a product of the revolution of 1688; for from thenceforward 'when ministers could not command a majority they retired from office.'[33] It 'will therefore be seen at a glance,' he continued, that in framing the constitution of 1791 for Canada, the British ministry 'had presumed that its social condition must resemble that of England before the revolution of 1688, and gave it accordingly very nearly the form of government existing there anterior to that period.' Canada 'had accordingly to go through the same revolutionary ordeal precisely, with the simple difference, that its rapid increase in population and wealth, brought about the crisis in a few years, which in England it had taken generations to mature.'

But in Upper Canada, McMullen contended, the evils of irresponsible government had been increased when the colony became a refuge for a host of poor gentlemen, half-pay officers, and others. Some became hangers-on of the administration; others 'retained ... as much of their land as ... they could cultivate to advantage, and sought to preserve by their exclusiveness the superiority, which they supposed their advantages of education, and the station which they had occupied hitherto in society, ought to entitle them to.'[34] Necessity drew these poor gentlemen together until they became a distinct party. 'Fostered by an irresponsible government ... it gradually acquired strength and influence: its members intermarried backwards and forwards among themselves, and at length it emerged into the full-blown, famous, Family Compact.'

Ranged against it, however, was another group of poor gentlemen who had adapted themselves to the colony without complaint. 'While they learned to wield the axe, and swing the cradle, with the energy and skill of the roughest backwoodsman, they retained their polished manners, their literary tastes, their love of the beautiful and the elegant, and thus exercised a most beneficial influence upon their rustic neighbours ... Their superior education, their well-bred manners, their more refined habits, raised them in the estimation of the rural population, who soon tacitly admitted a superiority, which would never have been conceded had it been more directly asserted.'[35] Thus 'as early as 1805,' he concluded, 'we find two distinct parties ... which very closely assimilated to the Tory and Whig parties in Great Britain, anterior to the revolution.'

The constraining effect of the Whig interpretation on the mind of McMullen could scarcely be more apparent. Yet he was not without originality. According to him, the basic cause of party conflict in Canada was resolved with the achievement of responsible government in 1840. Many other issues, to be sure, had agitated the colony over the years, and continued to agitate it after 1840; but, as he surveyed the scene in 1855, these seemed to have pretty well worked themselves out. 'Party bitterness,' he wrote, 'has disappeared and the line of demarcation between Conservatives and Reformers has so narrowed as to render it difficult to be discerned. In point of fact there are no political parties in the country as we write; and a coalition party, led by Sir Allan M'Nab, conduct [*sic*] the government of the country.'[36]

Intended as a careful, objective, indeed scientific account of the past, McMullen's history is a near-perfect example of the imaginative projection of myth, the pattern of which is quite clear. The reformers, like St George, had slain a fierce dragon, the family compact, to liberate responsible government, a fair lady, who had long languished in chains.

Louis Turcotte's *Le Canada sous l'union, 1841–1867* of 1871 is a much more carefully researched history than that of McMullen. Yet he too was much concerned with responsible government; not, to be sure, as the culmination of a momentous epoch, but as the beginning of an era in which one could observe 'les descendants des deux grandes nations qui président à la civilisation du monde, fraterniser ensemble, et réunir leurs efforts pour procurer le bien-être et la prospérité du pays.'[37] Like McMullen, Turcotte held that when England granted the constitution of 1840, 'elle concéda en même temps la forme de gouvernement généralement connu sous le nom de *gouvernement responsable*';[38] indeed, he believed it had been conceded in a dispatch written by the colonial secretary, Lord John Russell, on 16 October 1839.[39] But, in a confusing sort of way, he also equated it with the form of government that prevailed only after 1848 during the administration of Lord Elgin. The root of his confusion, of course, was that he followed a misleading gloss placed upon Russell's dispatch by the party of Lafontaine and Baldwin.

Russell had directed only that the principal offices of the Crown be held at pleasure, that ministers retire when motives of public policy might make such a change politically expedient. Governors were neither instructed to form ministries from majoritarian parties nor required invariably to accept the advice of their ministers. Turcotte knew this; and he was quite able to distinguish between the practice of government under Lord Sydenham and his immediate successors and that which prevailed after Elgin. As with so many others, however, he was completely unable to unscramble these distinctions from '*gouvernement responsable*.' That form of government, he thought, had been granted in 1840 but would only be applied 'dans toute sa plénitude' later.[40]

But, if Turcotte was confused by his sources, this was not the main source of a very similar confusion that prevailed in English Canada. At play here was a division of opinion between those who were culturally oriented with respect to the mother country and those who were territorially oriented with regard to the

British Empire. In the former camp were emigrants from the British Isles, like the Baldwins, who were primarily intent upon transplanting the institutions of their old home to their new; in the latter camp were long-established North Americans who harked back to the traditions of the United Empire Loyalists. So important was this division of opinion that it frequently overrode the Tory/Reform political division. Among reformers in the 1830s, and among both reformers and Tories after 1840, this division is reflected in a battle as to the meaning of 'responsible government.'

A fine example of a territorially oriented reformer is Egerton Ryerson, a Methodist leader of United Empire Loyalist descent. In the 1820s he had been one of the most effective antagonists of the administration of Sir Peregrine Maitland, which has so often been termed 'the family compact.' No less opposed to the fragmentation of the empire, however, he broke with radicals who seemed to favour separatist politics in the 1830s, rallied to the cause of Lieutenant-Governor Head in the elections of 1836, and did the same on behalf of Governor Metcalfe in 1844. His intervention in these latter elections is of particular interest to us here in that he then contended, against Baldwinite reformers, that Metcalfe's conduct of government was entirely in accord with the principles of responsible government.[41]

Ryerson's politics, however, seemed quite maverick to those who entertained the notion that responsible government simply meant parliamentary government as practised at Westminster. One such person was the Baldwinite leader, Sir Francis Hincks, who in his old age, in the late 1870s, set himself the task of correcting factual errors in Canadian history, of exposing the allegedly misguided views of old opponents like Ryerson, and of impressing his own view of the past upon historians. Through his own writings, but more especially through those of John Charles Dent, which he directly influenced, Hincks has had a lasting influence upon Canadian historical thought. Indeed, his influence upon historical thought is undoubtedly his most impressive political achievement.*

In contrast to other writers, Hincks was not at all concerned with the vexed question of just when responsible government was conceded to Canada. For in his view it was simply a right of which British subjects everywhere had long been possessed. This right had been recognized, to be sure, by the enlightened Lord Durham in the 1830s; but it had also been recognized back in the eighteenth century by the scarcely less enlightened Lieutenant-Governor John Graves Simcoe, who had assured the first legislators of Upper Canada that they were possessed of 'the very image and transcript of the British Constitution.'[42]

Within Hincks's own Anglo-Irish tradition, this point of view was very old; but it was not at all well understood outside that tradition. It was from this point of view that Hincks charged in 1877 that the colonial secretary, the Earl of Derby (then Edward Stanley), and Lord Metcalfe had sought to extinguish responsible government in the 1840s. But it was from a quite different, no less valid point of view that the aged Egerton Ryerson rejoined that 'the Earl of Derby had no more intention or desire to abolish Responsible Government in Canada than had Sir Francis Hincks himself.'[43] The total breakdown in communication between these two old reformers is further indicated by Hincks's pointlessly irrelevant reply to Ryerson. 'I am by no means unaware that the Earl of Derby, Lord Metcalfe and Dr. Ryerson, insisted that they were favorable to Responsible Government, but I can scarcely imagine that Dr. Ryerson, who lived

* See: Francis Hincks, *The Political History of Canada between 1840 and 1855* (Montreal 1877); *Reminiscence of His Public Life* (Montreal 1844). Hincks's influence upon J.C. Dent is indicated in his letters to that historian. See Elizabeth Nish, ed., 'How History Is Written,' *Revue du Centre D'Etudes de Québec* 2 (Apr. 1968) and G.H. Patterson, 'Dent, John Charles,' *Dictionary of Canadian Biography*, vol. 11 (Toronto 1982), 246–9.

so many years after that system had been honestly administered, could have believed that Lord Metcalfe entertained the same views on the subject as Lord Elgin.'[44]

V

From this discussion it should be evident that to entertain single, fixed concepts of the family compact and of responsible government is to be at least as far from appreciating their true function as was Hincks from having had a meeting of minds with Ryerson. Our purpose here, however, is not merely to reveal how the multiple meanings of these terms have led to much thinking and writing at cross purposes, but to relate these factors to the function of metaphor and myth.

For the past fifty years, the historian of religion Mircea Eliade observed in 1963, 'Western scholars have approached the study of myth from a viewpoint markedly different from ... that of the nineteenth century. Unlike their predecessors, who treated myth in the usual meaning of the word, that is as "fable," "invention," "fiction," they have accepted it as it was understood in the archaic societies, where, on the contrary, "myth" means "a true story" and, beyond that, "a story that is a most precious possession because it is sacred, exemplary, significant." '[45] Indeed, myth has come to be understood as at once illusory and significant as simple fiction is not. In this sense of the word, this chapter has been concerned with the development, permutations, and fragmentation of the story of the overthrow of the family compact and the triumph of responsible government. As embedded in Canadian history, this story partakes of the nature of myth.

But this chapter is also a study of formal causality, of the effects of the form of the myth and of its component forms. Shared myth is a means whereby societies legitimize themselves. It sanctions existing social orders, justifies status systems and power structures, and provides rationales for social and political institutions. Promoting the integration of societies, such myth contributes to group identities, cultural stability, and social harmony. Stories of the struggle for responsible government are generally mythic views of this sort.

Myth may equally well justify social and political revolution, however. And, underlying stories of the achievement of responsible government, centring on concepts of family compacts and court parties, is to be discerned myth of the latter type. Caught up by powerful mythologies of this sort, men have been led to rebellion, exile, and death.

Myth is a complex of symbols and images embedded in narrative. As distinguished from simple fiction, it often furnishes a pattern whereby the data of experience are ordered to be understood. In this regard it functions as metaphor, which is not literally true but which is much more than just a decorative device or imaginary pretence with no relation to reality.

As with metaphor, myth involves transfer of meaning, a highly selective transfer of associations from one context, or set of contexts, to another. Expressive of a poet's experience, metaphor is evocative of the reader's; and so it is with myth. Both metaphor and myth function as a sort of filter whereby certain features of a subject are ignored or suppressed while others are emphasized or distinctively organized.

Politicians, however, are seldom poets, and it is with political rather than poetic devices that we are concerned here. Yet poetry and politics have much in common. When Barnabas Bidwell, for example, applied the phrase 'family compact' to an understanding allegedly uniting his Federalist enemies in Massachusetts, he employed metaphor as surely as if he had declared his love to be a red, red rose. Involved here was a highly selective transfer of meaning from the European context of the *pacte de famille* to an American context of revolutionary republican politics. It was a figure/ground relationship, moreover – the figure of a monarchical family compact related to an American republican ground – that gave to the image its initial emotive force. Beyond this, the metaphor functioned long after it ceased to be recognized as such and after its early contexts were long forgotten. For, from start to finish, whether applied to small groups with family connections or to large ones without any, the term carried overtones of nepotism.

The expression 'responsible government,' on the other hand, was a symbol of a different order; for it had no such metaphoric function. It was scarcely less evocative, however, of a rich diversity of meaning. Initially its main opposite was 'family compact,' and from this relationship it derived much of its symbolic force. When applied to the politics of the 1840s, however, it began to be torn loose from its old opposite; but this, as we have seen, was a long, slow process, spanning several generations. In the work of writers like Stephen Leacock and Chester Martin responsible government, considered as *figure*, acquired a new *hidden ground*, the maintenance of the British Empire.

During the 1820s and 1830s in Upper Canada the balance of power shifted from governors and appointed councils to the popularly elected assembly. Within the latter body an opposition to the executive slowly took on fixed, coherent form and organized itself to fight elections on platforms of provincial rather than merely local issues. The shift from radical rhetoric of the 'court party' sort to 'compact' rhetoric corresponds with this shift. In response to the Reform Party, supporters of the executive in the assembly organized themselves along similar party lines.[46] Thus by 1840 it had become increasingly difficult for governors to formulate policy without taking into account the views of whatever party was dominant in the assembly. The old idea of a balanced constitution, nevertheless, was not quite undone.

After the union of 1840, however, the process of constitutional change was hastened. Colonial secretaries now instructed governors to appoint to their executive councils persons holding seats in the assembly, a change thought by many to mark the advent of responsible government. But governors were not obliged to make appointments on a basis of party standing in the house; nor were they necessarily obliged to take their ministers' collective advice. These last obstacles to majoritarian party dominance were overcome only in 1848; and this, according to others, marked the achievement of responsible government. What was at issue here was whether or not 'responsible government' implied complete autonomy, a question about which Canadians were then strongly divided.

To assail the wicked advisers of the Crown in the name of responsible government was one thing among nineteenth-century English Canadians; to seek to dismember the British Empire was quite another. Yet – many long arguments to the contrary – responsible government, as understood by Baldwinite reformers, was logically linked to *political*, if not *cultural* separation from the mother country. And political separation was necessarily linked to the further democratization of colonial government.

Like Egerton Ryerson, a majority of English Canadians were long opposed to political separation. The electorate spoke upon this issue as decisively as it ever spoke in the Upper Canadian elections of 1836; and it did so again during the Union in 1844. Beginning in the 1850s, imperially minded historians sought to resolve the conflict of imperial and democratic aspirations by way of the term 'responsible government' and its ambiguities, which subsumed several concepts. This is to be discerned in primitive form in the pages of J.M. McMullen; it attained its greatest elaboration in those of Chester Martin. In both instances history partook of myth, of myth that mediated a major contradiction in Canadian public opinion.

In the nineteenth and early twentieth century this myth was intensely meaningful, which is to say, borrowing the language of McLuhan, that it was archetypal. But this has ceased to be the case. By the mid-twentieth century, as we have seen, Donald Creighton, moved by the thought of Harold Innis, mockingly treated it as cliché. For over the course of time not only has the historiographical context shifted but so too has the larger Canadian social and political context changed. Symbolic meaning has been lost. By setting the figure in another ground meaning is restored, but it is of a very different sort.

SIX

COMPARISONS

I

Writing, Harold Innis observed, 'implied a decline in the power of expression and the creation of grooves which determined the channels of thought of readers and later writers.'[1] Delivered in a presidential address to the Royal Society of Canada in 1947, this remark in some ways anticipated Thomas S. Kuhn's *The Structure of Scientific Revolutions*, which was published fifteen years later.[2] So too did Innis's attempt at displacing Newtonian mechanical models of actuality with paradigms derived from more recent physics. Kuhn's book examined the way in which experimental evidence for new scientific theory is accumulated and assimilated to older mistaken, but not yet outmoded, models or paradigms. A paradigm he took to be a 'universally recognized scientific achievement that for a time provides model problems and solutions to a community of practitioners.'[3] The paradigms that he studied, such as the Ptolemaic, Copernican, and Newtonian models of the universe, were only slowly broken down by the accumulation of anomalies that initially were not recognized as such. Kuhn's scientific paradigms resemble some of the historiographic models – such as 'the Whig interpretation' – examined in previous chapters. They also resemble McLuhan's cliché/archetypes with respect to the manner in which their structure rises to human consciousness.

Compared to more orthodox scholars, Innis and McLuhan themselves were anomalies; and if their work has originality and value it is because of this. Their work may well be most valuable when compared to and contrasted with more orthodox scholarship. Their books, however, have tended to be either partially assimilated to conventional patterns of thought or else to be completely rejected. It is ironic that admirers of Innis have assimilated his thought to conventional patterns he was breaking away from. It is doubly ironic that he, a generalist *par excellence*, who repeatedly pointed to the danger of fragmenting

knowledge through specialization, has himself come to be cate-
gorized as a specialist, that is as a specialist in 'the field of
communications.' This has been accomplished by a shift in the
meaning of the word 'communications.' The category 'communications,' it has been assumed, comprised something quite
other than history or, at least, quite other than Canadian history.
Our problem here relates to the organization or categorization
of ideas.

Both Robert Adair, who was a hostile critic, and Donald
Creighton, who was sympathetic, thought of Innis as having
moved into categories of history that were not Canadian. Adair
criticized him severely for this. Had he moved into new fields
of *specialization*, Adair would have been right. But this was not
the case; that was the very opposite of what he was attempting.
Innis was not, and never tried to become, an Egyptologist,
classicist, medievalist, or whatever. He did, however, attempt to
make use of these 'monopolies' of knowledge. His concern was
to generalize from his own field of interest and to make use
of the work of other specialized scholars. Neither Adair nor
Creighton recognized that in the so-called late work Innis was
applying ideas derived from earlier studies of the St Lawrence
communications system; and neither appears to have appreciated what he thought about Newtonian mechanics, what he
understood by the 'mechanization' of language, and what he
meant by 'monopolies' of knowledge.

History, he thought, was not a clockwork. 'Mechanization,'
Innis wrote, 'has emphasized complexity and confusion; it has
been responsible for monopolies in the field of knowledge; and
it becomes extremely important to any civilization, if it is not to
succumb to the influence of this monopoly of knowledge, to
make some critical survey and report. The conditions of freedom of thought are in danger of being destroyed by science,
technology, and the mechanization of knowledge, and with
them, Western civilization.'[4] Mechanization of knowledge and

specialization, in other words, inhibited the mind from moving freely from one category of expertise to another. So too could other inappropriate categories of thought such as late work and early work. These latter concepts, of course, can be either appropriate or inappropriate depending upon context. They are inappropriate when applied to the thought of Innis; but they are the contrary when applied to that of some of his critics.

Adair and Creighton were of one mind with respect to Innis's graceless English prose and in this respect they were largely right. Innis never found it easy to translate discontinuous, analogical modes of thought into linearly sequential and logically ordered writing. But his way of thinking was his great strength. From it sprang originality. But it was here that communications broke down between him and his colleague Donald Creighton. Creighton, having steeped himself in the linearly organized work of English novelists and historians to the end of acquiring the art of narrative prose, found linearly organized thought forms easy, natural, and normative.

Creighton, who could declare that historical events were basically unique and therefore not comparable, and whose view of the course of historical events was linearly biased, was predisposed to assimilate only certain of the work of his friend. But, despite his comment about the impossibility of comparison, Creighton himself took comparative approaches to the data of history. It would really have been quite impossible for him to have thought about facts at all had he not done so. But it probably would not have crossed his mind that words, for example, might usefully be compared to rivers, or that to some sound purpose the policies of Egyptian pharoahs might be compared to those of Sir John A. Macdonald. Yet the pharoahs with their communications systems, like Macdonald with his, were preoccupied with a common problem, with what Innis defined as 'the problem of space,' even as Louis Riel and his Métis followers were preoccupied with what Innis termed 'a concern for time.'

Creighton did not see this. When he thought about history he tended to conceive of it essentially in terms of narrative sequence.

'There is a tension in narrative, as in life,' observed Robert Coover, a reviewer of Milorad Pavic's non-linearly organized *Dictionary of the Khazars*, 'between the sensation of time as a linear experience, one thing following sequentially (causally or not) upon another, and time as a patterning of interrelated experiences reflected upon as though it had a geography and could be mapped.'[5] This would not be a bad description of one of the major tensions in the late work of Innis. 'It is, in a sense,' Coover continued, 'the tension between future time, which, with its promise of death and its intransigent sequence of days and nights, bears down upon us remorselessly, and time past, which, if it can be said to exist at all, exists only in cranial space, in that sprawling, multilevel and often chaotic house of our memory.' He might have written 'house of our mind.' Time past, it is seldom remembered, exists only within the mind that reflects upon it. The essential question, then, is *how* it is reflected upon.

Time past can be structured and restructured within cranial space in many ways. Newton thought of time as absolute; Einstein conceived of it as relative. And it need not necessarily be imagined to be linearly patterned. T.S. Eliot wrote:

> *Time present and time past*
> *Are both perhaps present in time future,*
> *And time future contained in time past.*[6]

This, it may be remarked, is a long way from the sentimental diachronically organized concept of time that Creighton applied when interpreting the pub scene in *The Waste Land*. And the difference between the mind of T.S. Eliot and that of D.G. Creighton, contrary to the dictum of the latter, can only be revealed by a *comparison* of their writings, which is to say of historical data.

Comparisons are important. Innis's treatment of the Nile can, and should, be compared with his treatment of the St Lawrence, although the conclusions he drew from the two systems were by no means identical. It is of interest, however, that students of his work have never contrasted the two, which may well be a consequence of linearly organized patterns of thought. Consider, for example, this passage from the late work:

The flow of the long Nile river to the north and dissipation of its regular floods in the numerous channels of the delta provided a background for the development of artificial canals and dykes by which the valley might be widened and the water held at the height of the flood for irrigation. The length of the river with the downward flow and the delta, and a shifting economic development incidental to dependence on a single line of transportation militated against a compact government and a stable political organization.[7]

Here Innis was dealing with what McLuhan termed 'formal causality.' That is to say, he was dealing with the effects of the form of a river. If it now seems remarkable that historians of Canada reading this passage could fail to recall Innis's earlier treatment of the St Lawrence, it is no more remarkable than the fact that intelligent reviewers of *Empire and Communications* could conclude that it had nothing at all to do with either transportation or rivers.

The misperceptions of these readers are worthy of examination. To an extent they proceeded from Innis's peculiar way of expressing himself. They were due too to the fact that many readers, like the specialized Egyptologist V. Gordon Childe, were probably unfamiliar with the early work; and that others, like Creighton, who were familiar with it, had had the disadvantage of having read him book by book as each was published rather than initially considering his work as a whole. They were impressed by the difference of the new work rather than by its similarity. But misperceptions seem also to have proceeded from mental grooves and preconceived categories of thought – preconceived paradigms – that led these readers to think of Innis's work in inappropriate ways, indeed in inappropriate directions. History no more has linear direction than has the cosmos. Beyond this, their knowledge was classified in ways that blocked understanding. The history of Canada, they tended to think, was something other than the history of ancient Egypt; and 'communications' was something other than either. This fragmented their thinking and broke the late work of Innis away from his early work.

In contrast to Creighton, who tended to think the way he wrote, which is to say serially, Innis tended to write the way he thought, which is to say comparatively or analogically. This made him exasperating to most readers but of interest to Marshall McLuhan. Creighton tended to arrange new historical data in accord with ideas he already entertained. Innis, as McLuhan remarked, set new data in apposition to ideas he held in order to generate further new ideas. In contrast to the 'categorization' and 'classification' of ideas, this was a process of 'free association.' A reader confronted by one of Innis's more impenetrable texts is forced to engage in free association also, or else remain forever bewildered.

Like Innis, McLuhan mistrusted the classification of new data in conformity with old categories. This he held blocked new perception. And this was at the heart of his disagreement with Northrop Frye. In contrast to Innis, McLuhan had no difficulty writing linear, sequential, logically ordered prose whenever he wished. Apparently, however, he did not always want to do this. A long-time student of rhetoric, he at times employed rhetoric to his own peculiar ends. The final version of *From Cliché to Archetype* – which the novelist John Fowles found to be about as elegant and lucid as a barrel of tar – is an example of this. Significantly the first draft of the book, from which McLuhan departed most radically, was written as linearly and sequentially as any critic could demand. The *form* of the work would seem to have been altered to disrupt patterns of thought in readers' minds, to make them think in ways in which they were not predisposed to think, to generate new ideas by setting ideas in apposition to each other. Understandably many readers found this to be most irritating. They expected a book to conform to their way of thinking.

If Innis always more or less thought as he did, McLuhan seems to have consciously adopted the technique of juxtaposition much later in life; for by his own account he learned it from his studies of the symbolists. At any rate, some of his research notes read very much like the discontinuous content of Harold Innis's 'Idea File.' Consider, for example, this single page of unpublished 'research notes' for *From Cliché to Archetype*.

Apropos Yeats ladder 'Now with my ladder gone, I must lie down again.' (cf. disappearance of organization chart.) This means abandoning jobs and functions within the organization.
It's lying down on the job!

'In the foul rag and bone shop of the dean of Arts office'
'law and ordure'

re sit-in
'To lie down in the Dean of Arts office where all degrees begin!'

Any human association engenders repetitive actions of speech or ritual or of utility for survival. These are inseparable from the creation of consciousness.

The Eskimo lives with survival technologies, not service technologies

Consciousness depends necessarily therefore upon repetition
= quotation = cliché
Cliché is prior. It must precede archetype.

The processes of cognition and invention which creates
consciousness and survival technology is one of probing.

Robert Ardrey – *The Territorial Imperative*.[8]

Documents like this reflect modes of thought remarkably like
those of Innis. They also reflect a methodology quite different
from that employed by conventional scholars. These latter generally depart from accepted interpretation only when moved to
do so by compelling evidence. Which is to say they tend to fit
new historical data to conventional patterns. Does any of this,
however, relate to history as it is presently studied?

II

The methodology of Innis and McLuhan was certainly quite
different from that employed by nineteenth-century writers of
history. Early historians like John M. McMullen were as linearly
minded as it is perhaps possible to be. Moreover these historians
fitted data derived from the Canadian experience to a pattern
of English 'Whig history' that, serving as a paradigm, pre-
existed in their minds. But books like McMullen's, it may be
objected, have long been assigned to an historiographical scrap
heap. Read today by almost no one, they have ceased to have
any influence.

Nineteenth-century Canadian historians still have their uses,
however. When we read their work today, the paradigmatic
patterns of their thought and the structure of their interpretations are apparent. Comparison of the older work to more
recent scholarship can make otherwise hidden structures of that
same recent work visible. For purposes of illustration let us

compare the work of nineteenth-century historians with Gerald Craig's more recent *Upper Canada: The Formative Years*, which is a careful, thoughtful, scholarly, and entirely orthodox work with a great deal to commend it. Because of its merits, it is very useful and interesting when considered in the present context. For, despite the subtitle, it has nothing at all to do with what McLuhan termed 'formal causality.'

As we have noticed, no concept in the tangled history of Upper Canada has so structured fundamental, mythopoeic interpretations of the past as have the varying notions of the *form* 'family compact.' In treating the period 1791–1841, nineteenth-century writers – whose thought was informed by concepts of what Aristotle termed 'efficient causality' and of interpretations that Innis viewed as 'mechanical' – generally supposed that the very processes of political and constitutional change had received their dynamic from the despotic activities of a single family compact. Centred at York but extended throughout the whole colony of Upper Canada, it was thought to have given rise to early popular protest, to the emergence of a reform party in the 1820s, to rebellion in the 1830s, and to the final achievement of responsible government some time in the 1840s. It was, in short, a first mover of history. This was in essence a 'mechanical' explanation of the past employing concepts of 'efficient' causality.

In 1963 Gerald Craig to a great extent departed from such opinion both with respect to this family compact and with regard to the grievances to which it had allegedly given rise. But to an extent he also merely modified nineteenth-century opinion. 'This epithet,' he wrote with regard to the *form* 'family compact,' 'which came into use about 1828, had only a limited accuracy since, as Lord Durham later pointed out, its members were not all tied together by family connection, nor were they the ingrown, selfish, and reactionary group that the phrase was meant by their opponents to suggest.'[9] But Craig needed the expression whatever its limitations. 'The term has persisted,' he observed, 'and continues to be useful to describe the relatively small, tightly knit group of men who dominated the government of Upper Canada in the 1820's and to a somewhat lesser extent in the following decade.' Why he thought it continued to be useful he did not directly indicate; but his reason is to be discovered in earlier assertions. 'Our point of departure in understanding Upper Canada's descent, first into bitter and destructive political wrangling, and then into rebellion, must be some discussion of the term "Family Compact." ' He felt obliged to begin with the family compact as his 'point of departure' because his mind was still *informed* by the *form* and by related nineteenth-century paradigms, albeit in a very attenuated way. He had changed much of the *content* of nineteenth-century *forms*; but he retained nineteenth-century *structure*.

The Upper Canadian rebels of 1837 also entertained concepts of a family compact and of responsible government; but these were not those of Gerald Craig. Had the rebels shared Craig's opinions they would never have taken up arms. The rebels' concepts, misleading though they may have been, are significantly important to any historian seeking to discern the causes of their rising. These concepts had been mediated to the rebels not by Gerald Craig but by William Lyon Mackenzie and others of his party. This had been accomplished both orally and through the medium of newspapers. In other words what today would be termed 'disinformation' was a cause of the rebellion. Clearly we are dealing here with a problem in communications. The content of the terms used by Mackenzie would later be altered by historians; but the medium was the message, the terms themselves remained intact. The polar opposites of family compact and responsible government would continue to govern historical thinking.

To get outside this system is not easy. Indeed, if one considers only modern writers it is probably quite impossible. A better starting point is to understand that much nineteenth-century English-Canadian political discourse is of one of three types. There is a rhetoric of loyalty to the British Empire and a rhetoric of republicanism, both of them predating a rhetoric of responsible government by which the earlier rhetorics were eventually displaced or subsumed. One must further understand that, in the 1880s, the mainstream of Canadian historical explanation became Baldwinite. In its purest political form this language is to be discovered in the utterances of William Warren Baldwin and his son Robert and their followers, in the historical writings of the Baldwinite politician Sir Francis Hincks, and more particularly in the histories of John Charles Dent, a writer much influenced by Hincks.* This school presented the Baldwinite reformers as a party of moderate constitutionalists, loyal to the mother country, opposed, on the one hand, to the separatist republican followers of William Lyon Mackenzie and, on the other, to the reactionary and despotic family compact, which was associated with a series of equally reactionary and misguided governors. This school early displaced the rhetoric of republicanism, which was viewed by some as simply the language of democracy but by others as that of separatism and treason. For, if it seemed to speak the former popular language, it also seemed to speak the disloyal latter. And in time the rhetoric of responsible government also displaced the language of imperialism, which to some, for a time, it too had spoken. Generally speaking, writers of this latter period were trying to write what in this century has been termed 'consensus history.' These interpretations were shaped by the changing imperial and national contexts within which their authors lived.

Over the years archival research has greatly modified nineteenth-century interpretation. It was considerably modified in

---

* For a more detailed treatment of Dent and Hincks see my biography of John Charles Dent, *Dictionary of Canadian Biography*, vol. 11, 246–9.

1927 when Aileen Dunham published *Political Unrest in Upper Canada*; and it was again much modified by Gerald Craig in 1963. But, as here argued, some of the basic structure remained intact. To perceive this structure it is helpful to examine some views of history that have been displaced.

In seeking to account for the Rebellion of 1837 in Upper Canada, historians when sifting the evidence have generally focused upon the *content* of newspapers and other documents rather than adopting the 'formal' approach of Innis and McLuhan. They have examined the grievances of the rebels and have generally concluded that these were considerably less weighty than reformers like W.L. Mackenzie maintained. Their work in this regard is of real value. Apart from this they also suggested that the rebellion had an economic motivation, that a recession exacerbated political unrest. This is more problematic.

All these causes, however, are of the sort Aristotle termed 'efficient.' Insofar as they were grievances by which men were actuated, they were 'mechanical' in their operation. And, to an extent, they undoubtedly did operate in just this fashion. But none of these causes are of the complementary sort termed 'formal.' No one has looked for hidden grounds that shaped the rebellion and the minds of men and against which the rising might have appeared as figure. In short, no one has sought to explain the rebellion in terms of communications. To discover how this might be done, let us turn to a consideration of the effects of waterways, roads, and newspapers.

III

Let us begin not with the family compact but with the late eighteenth century, with the period that immediately followed the American War of Independence. At this time the forms 'family compact' and 'responsible government' were quite unknown to Upper Canadians. That being the case, in dealing with this period we must do what most historians of the colony have not done; we must forget all about them. The opposed cliché/archetypes then current derived from concepts of loyalty to king and empire and of republicanism. This ideological conflict, which was later masked by the literature of responsible government, must be kept very clearly in mind. For around such notions clustered the ideas and passions that really actuated the politics of the period.*

When first settled by refugees from the American War of Independence, Upper Canada was served by one dominant communications system, that of the St Lawrence–Great Lakes waterways. Most people were then completely oriented to this system, along the shores of which they were partially and very thinly settled. For the most part these settlers took up farmland from the Lower Canadian border to the shores of the Bay of Quinte on Lake Ontario. When their farms became productive, they became oriented to markets downriver in Montreal. Some less fortunate refugees, however, settled near the distant British garrisons at Niagara and Detroit. They were still on the waterfront, but these garrisons, not Montreal, furnished these farmers' first small markets. Markets in Montreal were then much too distant.

In 1793 two new communications systems began to be established; and these gave rise to forms of sectionalism. These were not waterways but roads, better described as barely passable tracks through the forest. By order of the lieutenant-governor, John Graves Simcoe, Dundas Street was cut through uninhabited wilderness to connect Burlington Bay at the west end of Lake Ontario with the Thames River near present-day Woodstock. From there the Thames flowed to the west about thirty

* In the index of *Upper Canada: The Formative Years* there are thirteen entries under the subject 'responsible government.' There is no subject 'republicanism.'

miles above Lake Erie to join Lake St Clair, which connected with both Lake Erie and Lake Huron. Along these roads Simcoe and his successors planted settlements. Simcoe's purpose, however, was primarily military. He wanted to secure a line of communications away from the American border that was not vulnerable to American attack. These military considerations were in many ways contradictory of what was then economic reality.

With the same military purpose in mind, Simcoe cut another track, this one called Yonge Street, north from York (Toronto) on Lake Ontario to Lake Simcoe, which was connected by waterways to Lake Huron. Along these two roads, and in areas sectionally affected by them, Simcoe and his successors established post-loyalist settlers. Prior to the War of 1812 most of these, but not all, were 'late loyalists' from the United States.

The areas affected by these two roads became the most politically disaffected regions in the province. Unrest was by no means confined to them; but here it was most intense. The problem was alluded to by Lieutenant-Governor Colborne in the early 1830s when he remarked that support for the radicals was greatest 'among settlers who entered the Province about 25 years ago from Pennsylvania, and the American population of the Townships of Markham and Vaughan in this country, connected with them ... Mechanics who lived for some time in the States before they settled in the province. The Colonial Advocate published by Mackenzie is taken in generally by the American population, and has made them discontented.'[10] It was from the communities served by Yonge Street, and the network of roads connected to it, that William Lyon Mackenzie gathered his rebels in 1837. It was down Yonge Street that they marched to strike at York. And it was from the London District, from Oxford, Norfolk, and Middlesex counties – whose politics were first disturbed by the Dundas Street–Thames River communications system – that other rebels marched to join Mackenzie.

These roads gave rise to conflicts of interest between settlers on the 'front' who were exclusively dependent upon the St Lawrence system and settlers in the 'rear' who were also dependent upon roads. Settlements on the front initially were more heavily populated and more fully developed than those in the rear. A majority of appointed magistrates, who when sitting in district courts of Quarter Session constituted local government, invariably came from the fronts. Throughout the colony conflicts of interest opened between settlers of the rear and those of the front; and rivalries opened between regional leaders. Electors of the rear, often in alliance with certain dissident electors of the front, who were disaffected from their magistrates for non-sectional reasons of their own, sought to elect to the House of assembly members hostile to unpopular magistrates. Sometimes these alliances were successful; at other times not. But in either event they generated bitter, rancorous, long-lasting political enmity.

Dundas Street was more divisive than was Yonge Street. The effects of the latter conform quite well to the Laurentian thesis as modified by J.M.S. Careless. He has treated what disciples of Frederick Jackson Turner regarded as 'frontiers' as 'hinterlands.' A Careless hinterland, in contrast to a Turnerian frontier, was not isolated from civilization but was symbiotically related to a metropolis. Yonge Street ran north-south connecting the hinterland of the rear with York, its emerging metropolis on the front. If the interests of this hinterland in some ways conflicted with those of York, in other respects the two complemented each other.

But such could not be said of the effects of Dundas Street. It ran not north-south but east-west. It connected the settlements of the rear not with those of the front on Lake Erie, where most of the magistrates resided, but with the Detroit River in the west and Lake Ontario in the east. It connected a region on Lake Ontario known as the Head of the Lake with a *potential* hinterland in the interior. This region on Lake Ontario included the emerging communities of Dundas, Ancaster, and Hamilton. For many years Dundas Street was barely passable by a man on horseback or by driven cattle. For some time it was unusable by horse-drawn wagons. Initially the interior was easier of access from Detroit in the west than from Lake Ontario in the east. By reason of this poor Dundas Street–Thames River communications system this isolated region in the interior in some ways more closely resembled a frontier of Turner than a hinterland of Careless. As a contemporary observer, the merchant Richard Cartwright, put it, Simcoe's plan for the development of the region was 'a scheme perfectly utopian, to which nature has opposed invincible obstacles; unless Mongolfier's [*sic*] ingenious invention could be adapted to practical purposes, and air balloons be converted in [*sic*] vehicles of commerce.'[11] In one significant way, however, this frontier differed from Turner's concept; for it was a frontier in desperate search of a metropolis. Eventually this isolated region became the hinterland of the Head of the Lake on Lake Ontario, leaving its developing economy unrelated to, indeed antagonistic to, that of the Lake Erie settlements to the south where control of local government was long lodged.

The settlers of the interior were for the most part 'late loyalists.' The officials of the front of Norfolk County with whom they first came into conflict were largely United Empire Loyalists. Later those of the rear also came into conflict with Colonel Thomas Talbot, a powerful aristocrat who settled the front of Middlesex County.

The region served by the Dundas Street–Thames River system became a hotbed of discontent that found expression in republican forms of protest. In 1807 the district clerk of the peace, Thomas Welch, writing of the 'late loyalists' of the rear noted that these people constituted 'nine out of ten of the inhabitants of the County of Oxford and part of the County of Middlesex.' These folk, he added, 'do keep the fourth of July annually in the same manner (firing excepted) as we subjects do the 4th of June [George III's birthday] ... they may however be well enough provided we have no war with the United States, but Should we unfortunately be plunged into a War ... the people above alluded to ... under the cloak of Subjects would (in my opinion – and in that opinion I am in no way Singular) be much to be dreaded.'[12] Welch was not unduly alarmed, as events attending the War of 1812 soon demonstrated.

The Dundas Street–Thames River communications system may or may not help explain in part the complex motivations of William Willcocks, the most famous of the traitors of the War of 1812. Willcocks was not a 'late loyalist' but an immigrant from Ireland who became prominent in opposition to the provincial executive. This was partly by reason of his peculiar Irish Whig ideology, but was more largely due to a frustrated search for patronage. During the war Willcocks raised and commanded a unit of about two hundred and fifty expatriate Upper Canadians known as the Company of Canadian Volunteers that raided into the colony from the United States.*

It is unlikely that Willcocks's more compelling motivations arose from the Dundas Street–Thames River communications system, and it is certainly possible that none of them did. Nonetheless two things do connect him with it. First, it cut directly across his riding of Lincoln 1st and Haldimand, which extended to the Indian reserve on the Grand River. Second, if what is

---

* The most recent study of Willcocks is Elwood H. Jones, 'Joseph Willcocks,' *Dictionary of Canadian Biography*, vol. 5 (Toronto 1983), 854–9. For Willcocks's Irish ideology, see my 'Whiggery, Nationality and the Upper Canadian Reform Tradition,' *Canadian Historical Review* 56 (Mar. 1975).

known of his personal interests appear not to have been directly affected by Dundas Street, the same cannot be said of his closest political and military associates.

To the west of Willcocks's riding was the county of Oxford, which, along with Norfolk and Middlesex, made up the District of London. There on Dundas Street lived Benajah Mallory. He became a major in the Canadian Volunteers and its commander upon the death of Willcocks.* Mallory had long engaged in fierce conflicts with district officialdom from the front of Norfork. In 1804 he was elected to the assembly as their opponent; and he was re-elected in 1808. In 1812, however, he was defeated, by reason of the poll's relocation to Middlesex and because of the votes of Colonel Talbot's settlers in Middlesex.

Also in the Volunteers was Abraham Markle who had interests at the Head of the Lake in Ancaster.† Markle was elected to the assembly for the riding of Saltfleet, Ancaster, and the West Riding of York in 1812. He soon became a captain in the Volunteers.

Apart from Willcocks, Mallory, and Markle, the most prominent of the Canadian Volunteers were Ebenezer Allan, Andrew Westbrook, and Simon Xelotes Watson.‡ These individuals all had interests related to the Thames River, of which Dundas Street was an extension. Allan had been granted 2,000 acres of land in Delaware township some forty miles up the Thames from Moraviantown. He had also been promised 200 acres for every settler he brought into the province. Westbrook and

* The most recent work on Mallory is Robert L. Fraser's study in the *Dictionary of Canadian Biography*, vol. 8, 606–9.

† For Markle, again see Robert L. Fraser, *Dictionary of Canadian Biography*, vol. 6, 488–91.

‡ For Allan, see Daniel J. Brock, *Dictionary of Canadian Biography*, vol. 5, 13–15; for Westbrook, see D.R. Beasley, vol. 6, 808–9. There are no recent studies of Watson.

Watson were both neighbours of Allan. All three men had come into conflict with Colonel Talbot.

The region from which these Volunteers emerged had a continuing history of republican radicalism that it would be tedious to trace in any detail here. It should, however, be taken account of by anyone seeking to explain the outbreak of rebellion in 1837. For the leader of that rebellion, Dr Charles Duncombe, represented Mallory's old county of Oxford, as did his fellow member the rebel Robert Alway. The Dundas Street–Thames River communications system moreover initially generated the radicalism of Dr John Rolph who was associated with the Mackenzie rising on Yonge Street.

It happened this way. In 1824 Rolph resided in the front of Middlesex County where he lived on very good terms with Colonel Talbot. Rolph wanted the colonel's support in being elected to the House of Assembly. Unfortunately the two incumbent members, Mahlon Burwell and Henry Bostwick, had Talbot's confidence. An opposition to these men, however, headed by a Captain John Mathews, emerged in the rear. Seeking to unite the voters of the rear with those of someone from the front, Mathews joined forces with Rolph.

Since Burwell, Bostwick, and Rolph were all from the front, this threatened fatally to split the vote of the front. In an attempt at avoiding this outcome one of the Talbot-supported candidates, Bostwick, retired from the contest on polling day. But this was to no effect. Rolph headed the polls followed by Mathews; and Talbot's man, Burwell, was defeated. Soon after this, Rolph, who had undoubtedly alienated old friends from the front, united with radical members of the assembly.*

* I have treated Middlesex politics and Rolph's role in them in considerable detail in chapter 1 of 'Studies in Elections and Public Opinion in Upper Canada' (unpublished PHD dissertation, University of Toronto 1969).

It would be quite mistaken, however, to understand the politics of the District of London only in terms of underlying sectionalism. The fact that Rolph's majority was obtained by a *union* of electors from front and rear is indicative of this. There were a great many other complicating factors at play in the district.

One of these was the emergence of yet another communications system. This was Kettle Creek, which, in contrast to the Thames River, flowed not east-west but north-south into Lake Erie. To be more precise, it flowed from the hamlet of St Thomas in the interior to Port Stanley on the lake. Kettle Creek tapped the grain supplies of the interior. So too did the Thames, which, relative to the Head of the Lake, was not too far from the St Thomas system. In the 1820s and 1830s, before the coming of railroads, barges on Kettle Creek promised to afford a better way of shipping flour and grain than did horse-drawn wagons on Dundas Street. The proposed construction of the Welland Canal to overcome obstacles on the Niagara River, the waterway joining lakes Erie and Ontario, also seemed to promise much for the Kettle Creek route. Eventually, of course, a railroad would reinforce or replace the Dundas Street – Thames River connection; but this was then unknown.

In these same years the demographic *ground* from which the politics of the 1830s would emerge as *figure* changed. Prior to the War of 1812 the population of the colony was mostly made up of Loyalists and late loyalists, which is to say it was primarily American. With the final defeat of Napoleon, however, the sea lanes from Great Britain were reopened. Thereafter the early American population of the colony was slowly submerged by thousands of settlers from England, Scotland, and Ireland. These were the people who opened up the rich farmlands in the western interior. And it was this settlement of the interior that made the waterways that penetrated it of corresponding interest to various merchants and millers. These waterways and their harbours were all in need of improvement; and this made a voice in government vitally important to merchants and millers.

In 1828 the village of St Thomas on Kettle Creek scarcely existed. It then contained only sixteen houses, one store, and a distillery owned by the firm of Hamilton and Warren. In that year, however, Colonel James Hamilton, who had been actively trying to persuade the government to dredge a harbour at Port Stanley, unsuccessfully stood for election. He had run in alliance with Colonel Talbot's successful candidate, Mahlon Burwell; but from this one should not conclude that their interests were identical. The interests of merchants were not those of Talbot and his farmer settlers. 'The *Jews* of merchants of the Talbot settlement,' observed the colonel, 'will make their fortunes at the expense of my industrious farmers, having given but 4 yorkers a bushel for wheat, and Hamilton and Warren have taken in ... near 20,000 bushels, most part of which for old debts, on which they no doubt had a profit of 700 per cent.'[13] Soon the conflict of the interests of the agrarian Talbot settlement and those of St Thomas merchants became more acute.

By the early 1830s several new merchants who dreamed large dreams of a commercial empire of Kettle Creek moved to St Thomas. There they established a newspaper, *The Liberal*. This journal, which was intended to promote the election of candidates supportive of local mercantile ambition and opposed to Colonel Talbot's candidates, had the same sort of formative effects upon public opinion in the London District that W.L. Mackenzie's *Colonial Advocate* and *Constitution* had along Yonge Street.

Marshall McLuhan has observed that modern newspapers like the *New York Times* contain a mosaic of unrelated reports united only by a common dateline. The same thing most certainly could not be said of the newspapers of Upper Canada, the political content of which was entirely unified. The content of the *Colonial Advocate*, for example, was united by the fiery mind and personality of its editor, W.L. Mackenzie, of which it was very much an extension. The content of *The Liberal* likewise was directed to the economic and political objectives of its owners.

The effects of these newspapers were very different from the effects of the modern daily press. They were weekly publications; and they were bitterly partisan. In the absence of modern alternative forms of communication, like radio and television, politicians found it difficult to make replies to political attacks. The only way was to establish a press of one's own; but this was not very effective. Very few readers subscribed to more than one newspaper; and with the passage of a week even fewer could accurately recall what was being replied to. The majority of the populace did not subscribe to newspapers at all. But the content of these papers passed to them by word of mouth in what was doubtless impassioned and probably distorted form. Distortions of this sort, which McLuhan insisted were part of a communications system, are important to any understanding of the politics of the period and of the people who formed their opinions from the system. All these factors made for a politics of extremism.

The St Thomas *Liberal*, which was first edited by Asahel Lewis,* and later by the rebel sympathizer John Talbot, appears to have been owned by Lewis, the merchants Lucius Bigelow, Josiah Goodhue, and Bela Shaw, and by forty-six smaller shareholders who were scattered through Middlesex County. Bigelow, Goodhue, and Shaw were of recent American origin; and Lewis was also. Little is known of the smaller shareholders, but they were probably persons hostile to the elected members for non-mercantile reasons.

Perhaps the most interesting aspect of the activities of this

---

* I have treated Lewis and the *Liberal* in the *Dictionary of Canadian Biography*, vol. 6, 399–400.

group is their manipulation of language to the end of shaping public opinion. These politicians were part of the emerging provincial Reform Party yet, curiously, called themselves not Reformers but Liberals. The term is as significant as it is curious. It of course did not come from the British Liberal Party, the father of which, William Ewart Gladstone, was then just on the point of entering English politics as a Tory. It did come from the Parliament at Westminster. There it meant a ministerialist too advanced to be called a Whig but not sufficiently advanced to be called a radical.* The Liberals of St Thomas were convinced republicans and their 'liberalism' was much informed by republicanism; but many of the homesick new settlers from the 'old country,' who now were enfranchised, were not inclined to separate from their mother country. Large numbers of these new voters were now settled in the rear.

Lewis and his associates were confronted with the hard reality that Middlesex, along with a majority of other ridings, had returned Tories to the Assembly in the general election of 1830. As merchants they were not particularly popular with farmers, and as American republicans they were not very attractive to many recently arrived immigrants. A pseudonymous 'Algernon Sydney' put it this way: 'most of the Emigrants who have arrived on our shores during the past two seasons, were Reformers in England – they brought with them here Liberal principles and liberal feelings, but so nicely have the government and the York gentry arranged matters, that they are able in a great majority of instances, effectually to smother all such sentiments ...'[14] The

---

* 'As a party the ministerialists were called and called themselves Reformers. The designation signified either the party which in the past had carried out the Reform of 1832 or the party whose programme for the future was a programme of reform. It was still the official designation of the party at the General Election of 1837 and 1841, although in newspaper articles the term Liberal tended to supplant the term Reformer.' (Elie Halévy, *The Triumph of Reform 1830–1841*, trans. E.I. Watkin, London 1927, 180n)

St Thomas merchants were in search of the votes of these immigrants, to which end they called themselves 'Liberals.' To this extent the electorate may be said to have had a formative influence upon the content of the *Liberal*. To the same *local* political end the columns of the paper were filled with standard *provincial* reform grievances.

In focusing upon local rather than provincial issues we have taken little account of the staple reform content of the *Liberal*. The effects of the paper are more interesting. Something of its formative impact is suggested by the fact that its candidates were returned in the general election of 1836, an election in which Tories elsewhere swept the province. It also had an interesting effect upon its local opponents. One of these, Alexander Ross, transmitted to the lieutenant-governor's private secretary a copy of 'what our precious agitators call the British constitution.' Distinguishing between the word 'liberal' and what it signified, he remarked: 'This vile stuff is a specimen of the jargon with which the party endeavours to wile our simple minded yeomanry into the gulphs of treason and destruction ... The title *liberal* given to the said pages furnishes a fair example of the singular application of words in which the party delight so much. They have certainly made no small progress in the art of perverting language.'[15] Here then is another usually unnoticed cause of the rebellion of 1837. The *Liberal*, insofar as it was a shaper of public opinion, would seem to have been a 'formal' cause of the rebellion. Certainly it was a formal cause of the outcome of the election of 1836.

In treating that election we have deliberately avoided mentioning the 'issues' over which it was fought. This is not intended to suggest that issues were unimportant; they were not. What was intended was to point to certain underlying causes that concentration upon particular issues has tended to obscure.

IV

The political economist and humorist Stephen Leacock was a close observer of Canadian politics and politicians. In many ways his humorous caricatures of Mariposans are more revealing than his very conventional biographies of Baldwin, Lafontaine, and Hincks. Indeed, they would seem to cast light upon those biographies. It is curious, and probably significant, that the solemn, portentous, and apparently entirely humourless *Baldwin, Lafontaine, Hincks: Responsible Government* was written by the same very humorous sceptic who penned 'The Great Election in Missinaba County.'

Leacock too had his models. His *Sunshine Sketches of a Little Town* derived from the real life of the citizenry of the small town of Orillia. Of this work, however, he wrote: 'I must disclaim at once all intention of trying to do anything so ridiculously easy as writing about a real place and real people. Mariposa is not a real town. On the contrary, it is about seventy or eighty of them. You may find them all the way from Lake Superior to the sea, with the same square streets and the same maple trees and the same churches and hotels, and everywhere the sunshine of the land of hope.'[16] Mariposa, it appeared, might even be St Thomas. He also claimed that his characters were not drawn from single models but were created from composites.

In all probability these lines were written to avoid giving direct offence to the people of Orillia. In this, however, Leacock failed; for they recognized themselves at once and were outraged. But there is a larger truth to his contention. It is from the universality of his creations, not their particularity, that they derive their archetypal character. Although suggested by Orillia, Mariposa was Leacock's comic metaphor for English Canada at large.

Every humorist, according to Marshall McLuhan, has a griev-

ance and every joke masks a grievance. If this be true Leacock's
grievance had something to do with a provincial Canada viewed
by a humorous, early-twentieth-century, imperially minded
political economist. In this regard it is instructive to recall what
this particular political economist made of the general election
of 1891, when Sir John A. Macdonald, giving expression to a
bias of time, fought and won it with the slogan: 'A British Subject
I was born: a British Subject I will die.'

Leacock really did not know a great deal about this election.
Indeed he only knew that it was a huge election and that on it
'turned issues of the most tremendous importance, such as
whether or not Mariposa should become part of the United
States, and whether the flag that had waved over the school
house at Tecumseh Township for ten centuries should be tram-
pled under the hoof of an alien invader, and whether Britons
should be slaves, and whether Canadians should be Britons,
and whether the farming class would prove themselves Canadians, and tremendous questions of that kind.'[17] Of particular
interest is Leacock's view of the electorate that grappled with
these momentous issues.

Let me begin at the beginning. Everybody in Mariposa is either a
Liberal or a Conservative or else is both ... These people get from long
training such a swift penetrating insight into national issues that they
can decide the most complicated question in four seconds: in fact just
as soon as they grab the city papers out of the morning mail, they know
the whole solution of any problem you can put to them. There are
other people whose aim is to be broad-minded and judicious and
who vote Liberal or Conservative according to their judgment of the
questions of the day. If their judgment of these questions tells them
that there is something in it for them in voting Liberal, then they do
so. But if not, they refuse to be the slaves of a party or the henchmen
of any political leader. So that anybody looking for henches has got to
keep away from them.[18]

These perceptive and principled electors whose minds had been informed by newspapers eventually returned Josh Smith, an astutely conniving hotel owner who, although he could not read, was clearly the smartest man in town.

To this historian, although apparently not to Leacock, cunning, manipulative Josh Smith bears more than a passing resemblance to Francis Hincks. In 1851, for example, Hincks contrived to secure the support of the radical Clear Grit party by bringing two of its leaders, John Rolph and Malcolm Cameron, into his then precarious ministry. According to the Toronto *Globe* Rolph was 'notoriously destitute of those methodical business habits, and that faculty of attention to minutiae, which are so obviously necessary in the Crown Lands Commissioner.' As for Cameron, he was a cloddish boor who 'we should say did not possess in a remarkable manner those graces of demeanour which might be supposed to compensate the country for the £800 annually to be paid him to sit at the top of a table doing *nothing*.' Mocking the Grits for having traded their principles for two insignificant offices, the *Globe* hailed the machiavellian skill of Hincks. 'Ah, Francis, Francis! – it was very cruel of you to slaughter the blustering Grits in this most murderous fashion! What a spectacle do they present! You have kicked them, cuffed them, spat upon them for two years past – and here you are dragging their chiefs through the mire at your chariot wheels.'[19] There is a notable lack of sunshine here. The hand of George Brown was a good deal heavier than that of Stephen Leacock. But, for all of that, one might almost believe one was back in Mariposa. And any biographer of Hincks should have been familiar with this sort of journalism.

When thinking about Leacock the political scientist one does well to recall that while the *Sunshine Sketches* was a book about Mariposans, *Baldwin, Lafontaine, Hincks: Responsible Government* figuratively speaking was addressed to Mariposans. One must also keep in mind that Leacock was writing in the first decade of the twentieth century. This was before the time of Lytton Strachey. It was a time when eminent Victorians like Sir Francis Hincks were usually treated by biographers as statesmen and not as shifty, contriving politicans. One certainly would not expect Leacock to caricature these worthies. On the other hand, however, characterization is so lacking in *Baldwin, Lafontaine, Hincks: Responsible Government* that Leacock himself commented upon it. 'In the present volume,' he wrote, 'the narrative of personal biography is subordinated to the record of political achievement.'

The name of Robert Baldwin and that of his distinguished colleague Louis Lafontaine will always be associated with the words responsible government. Baldwin was frequently derided by his contemporaries as a 'man of one idea.' Time has shown that this 'one idea' of Robert Baldwin, – the conception of responsible government, – has proved the corner-stone of the British imperial system. It is fitting, therefore, that this brief account of the political career of Robert Baldwin and his associates should centre round the evolution of responsible government in the province of Canada.[20]

This, one suspects, was the purest moonshine. One of Leacock's favourite literary forms was parody.

The way a man reads a book may well be related to the way he writes a book. Stephen Leacock read a book like this:

In writing about detective stories ... I stated that, for me it wasn't necessary for the writer of such a story to put into his book a plan of the house that was the scene of the murder. I said that I carried in my head ... a plan of the house already made, cut up into bedrooms, with a passage-way, and one 'bath' (for everybody) and a shape like a sausage lying loose in one room and marked 'body ...'

I had no sooner written this than I realized that it was only one sample of the quantity of junk which any reader carries round in his mind, ready to use, like the 'sets' of a repertory theatre ...

It's the same with the characters. We all have a stock of them ready
for use like marionettes in a child's theatre. For example a 'benevolent
old gentleman' – what a peach he seemed when we first read of him at
twelve; what a nut now. You see no new benevolent old gentleman can
get a chance with us; the minute the author names him we say 'Right
oh!' and substitute our own.[21]

Leacock, it would appear, was discussing cliché/archetypes.

It would also appear that what he had to say on the subject
does not apply to his own *Sunshine Sketches*. One cannot, for
example, easily substitute one's own imagined Josh Smith for
Leacock's creation.

If, then, you feel that you know the town well enough to be admitted
to the inner life and movement of it, walk down this June afternoon
halfway down the Main Street – or, if you like, halfway up from the
wharf – to where Mr. Smith is standing at the door of his hostelry. You
will feel as you draw near that it is no ordinary man that you approach.
It is not alone the huge bulk of Mr. Smith (two hundred and eighty
pounds as tested on Netley's scales). It is not merely his costume,
though the chequered waistcoat of dark blue with a flowered pattern
forms, with his shepherd's plaid trousers, his grey spats and patent-
leather boots, a colour scheme of no mean order. Nor is it merely Mr.
Smith's finely mottled face. The face, no doubt, is a notable one –
solemn, inexpressible, unreadable, the face of the heaven-born hotel
keeper. It is more than that. It is the strange dominating personality
of the man that somehow holds you captive. I know nothing in history
to compare with the position of Mr. Smith among those who drink
over his bar, except, though in a lesser degree, the relation of the
Emperor Napoleon to the Imperial Guard.[22]

One cannot easily substitute one's own imagined image of Mr
Smith for that of Leacock; not even one's own imagined image
of machiavellian but lean old Francis Hincks. The same thing,
however, cannot be said of certain moonshine sketches of those

benevolent old gentlemen 'Robert Responsible-Government,' 'Francis Responsible-Government,' and that other mechanical bride 'Louis Hippolyte Gouvernement-Responsable.'

But, it might be objected, Leacock was writing circa 1907; *Baldwin, Lafontaine, Hincks: Responsible Government* was merely a conventional interpretation of the times. This objection indeed has merit. The book was entirely conventional; but it would not seem to have been merely that. Leacock was promoting a particular version of responsible government, an imperially oriented version, to which end anything resembling a sunshine sketch of Francis Hincks or of any other reformer would have been counter-productive to say the least.

In 1907, however, scholars were not as naive as their books sometimes seem to suggest. Leacock's friend William Dawson LeSueur was a strong-minded historian who was most unfavourably impressed by *Baldwin, Lafontaine, Hincks: Responsible Government*. 'A few words now on the question of Responsible Government,' he scolded:

I quite recognize that a book can be written on the lines of yours that will give satisfaction to a large section of the public, but my feeling was that, in dealing with Baldwin, Lafontaine, and Hincks, an opportunity was afforded for doing something a little better than repeating that twice told tale, however, skillfully the retelling might be done. I was hoping for a book that would make, or if that is impossible, would at least invite people to think dispassionately and unconventionally on the course of Canadian history. Considering the point at which we have arrived in our political development, and the many evils which have fastened themselves on our political system, the time is ripe for a very critical treatment of our political conventions and catch words. The note of your book, on the other hand, is the note of finality. 'It is finished – we have Responsible Government.' Yes we have 'responsible government' and corruption has so enlarged itself that witnesses in the box almost jeer at the magistrate who enquires into their inequities, and a horrible cynicism in regard to every profession of political virtue has taken solid possession of a very large portion of the community. Is this the time to persuade people that their welfare is accomplished, and that they may sit down in peace under Responsible Government as under a combination vine and fig tree? I do not say you distinctly say so in your book, but I do say that you have done it negatively by missing a great opportunity of presenting certain questions as open questions, instead of as eternally settled ones. It is the note of enquiry, that note of what Balfour* calls 'philosophic doubt,' that I miss in a book that gave exceptional advantage – far more than the book I am writing – for introducing it† ...[23]

LeSueur was shrewd and perceptive. In associating the achievement of responsible government with party patronage and political corruption he was as sceptical about politicians and the electorate as was Leacock about his Mariposans. But he does not seem to have taken into account Leacock's imperialism. There was no way Leacock would have written the sort of book LeSueur had in mind.

In 1907 Leacock was either the prisoner of a paradigm and unable to see things as clearly as LeSueur, or else for purposes of his own he deliberately chose to write within a particular convention. One suspects that the latter was the case. But, in any event, if responsible government were indeed a 'cornerstone' of the British Empire, he would have been one of the last men in the Dominion to seek to dislodge it.

---

* The reference is to A.J. Balfour, *The Foundations of Belief* (London 1895).

† The reference is to LeSueur's biography of W.L. Mackenzie. Written between 1907 and 1908, it was suppressed for many years by reason of action taken by Mackenzie's grandson, William Lyon Mackenzie King, then a deputy minister of labour in the Laurier government, who would later himself become prime minister of Canada. In 1979, however, it was published as edited and introduced by A.B. McKillop. See *William Dawson LeSueur, William Lyon Mackenzie: A Reinterpretation* (Toronto 1979).

By 1926 Leacock seems to have lost interest in responsible government. In that year a revised edition of *Baldwin, Lafontaine, Hincks* was published. But it was revised not by him but by W.P.M. Kennedy, who thanked Professor Leacock 'for his courteous permission to deal as I wished with his work.'[24] Perhaps Kennedy's most interesting revision had to do with the book's title. On the title page this now became *Mackenzie, Baldwin, Lafontaine, Hincks*, while on the spine of the volume the pantheon of statesman reformers was even further enlarged. Here the title read: *The Struggle for Responsible Government: Mackenzie, Baldwin, Lafontaine, Hincks, Papineau, Cartier*.

Whatever Leacock thought or did not think of responsible government, his concern for the British Empire endured; and the Statute of Westminster came as a great blow to him. Writing of this document in 1940, he observed:

Yet the Statute of Westminster is, after all, only the newest riddle of the Sphinx. The Americans ... had their own riddle of the Sphinx for seventy years, in the Constitution as adopted in 1789. As far as the right of secession was concerned, it remained, as Goldwin Smith once said, a 'Delphic oracle.' The Americans finally killed 'States' Rights' with the sword, and buried it under constitutional amendments ...

For us in the British Empire the future is veiled. We can only hope and believe. It might perhaps have been wiser if the Statute of Westminster had declared the British Empire indissoluble. The fact is that the organic union of its structure is strong. The King's subjects ... are closely held together, not by compacts of government but by the affections and antecedents of uncounted millions. Separation by a mere majority vote could never tear away a dominion from the Empire. Perhaps it would have been better to say so. But perhaps not; sleeping dogs, even British bulldogs, are best left alone. Or would it have been better to have put into the statute an explicit declaration that any of the 'autonomous commonwealths' could secede at will? Again perhaps not; the dog might wake up.[25]

Mariposans, like sleeping dogs, it seemed, were best left undisturbed.

V

This concluding chapter, like the entire book, has been concerned with models, myths, and metaphors, with the categorization of ideas, and with cliché/archetypes. It has also been concerned with a Canadian context that initially generated interest in the transformation and breakdown of empires and the emergence of nation states.

This context or ground can be traced back to the 1760s when United Empire Loyalists first took up their pens to contend with American separatists. After the War of Independence the dispute continued within the remaining colonies of British North America, fought out between imperialists and autonomists. This division generated the several interpretations of 'responsible government' that, from a historiographical point of view, opened with the disputes of Francis Hincks and Egerton Ryerson. The autonomist interpretation was established in the 1880s by Hincks and the historian John Charles Dent. This form was seized from the autonomists in the 1890s by imperialists like William Kingsford who contended that colonial liberty and imperial unity had been entirely reconciled by responsible government; and as we have seen Stephen Leacock was still carrying the ball in the next decade. But by the 1920s and 1930s the responsible government game was drawing to a close. The term, it is true, lingered on in historical discourse as a cliché; but historians' interests were moving elsewhere.

They were moving into the field of communications, which seemed to relate better to the problems of empire. This was true with respect to Donald Creighton, whose empire of the St Lawrence and dominion of the north were bound together by communications systems. But it was even more true of Harold

Innis. The difference between Innis and Creighton in this regard is once more revealed by the latter's reaction to the Beit Lectures that Innis delivered at Oxford and of which *Empire and Communications* became the printed form. 'The Beit Lectures, six in number,' wrote Creighton,

were a more serious affair [than had been the Stamp Lectures]. The assignment obviously called for a more extended effort; and the terms of the fund required 'a subject in the economic history of the British Empire'. But Innis was no longer very interested in any subject which lay comfortably inside the economic history of the British Empire. The only major work which he had in contemplation was a history of the written and spoken word, not only in the British Empire, but also in Graeco-Roman civilization, and in the empires of Babylonia and Egypt. He may have tried, for a brief while at least, to accommodate himself more literally to the requirements of the Beit Fund; but this attempt was fairly quickly abandoned, and he decided to cram the essence of his long, elaborate historical argument on communications within the straining limits of six academic discourses.[26]

This, however, was not exactly the way Innis perceived his problem. He seems to have thought it impossible to adopt the categories that Creighton and presumably those who had endowed the Beit fund accepted as normative, one of which was 'the economic history of the British Empire.' 'We are immediately faced with the very great, perhaps insuperable, obstacle,' he wrote, 'of attempting ... to appraise economic considerations by the use of tools that are in themselves products of economic considerations.'[27] In treating the economic history of the British Empire he thought his main problem was to equip himself with proper tools, to which end he took a comparative approach to the Empire.

In this regard it is useful to recall the criticism Innis directed at Sir James Jeans's *Physics and Philosophy*. The title, he remarked, along with the headings of chapters suggested a fundamental weakness. 'Philosophy is concerned with the whole range of knowledge including physics and cannot be regarded as separate from physics or as subordinate to it as the title implies. The changing place of physics in philosophy would have been a title implying a proper and more respectful relationship.'[28] Precisely the same criticism, it would appear, could be directed at the title of this present book, *History and Communications*. For as Innis would have been the first to observe, history *is* communications. That observation, however, takes us back to the point where this book began.

AFTERWORD

I

In books like this, writers usually explain their intentions in introductions. This is not the case here; this book has no introduction. Its afterword, however, might well seem to resemble one. For among other things it explains how the book came to be written, how it was written, and what it was intended to accomplish. But it is not an introduction in that it is meant to be read after the arguments in the main body of the text have been examined.

Some readers might conclude that this afterword, in point of fact, is really an introduction, and that in an eccentric McLuhanite fashion it appears at the end of the book even as in *From Cliché to Archetype* the introduction appears in the middle. Such is not the case. McLuhan was attempting to derail the reader from the smooth and uniform progress that is typographic order, to encourage the reader to read non-sequentially, to juxtapose the contents of the book at random, to dislocate the mind into perceiving new meaning.

Nothing could be further from my purpose here. While there is a good deal to be said in favour of McLuhan's techniques, it is also true that some of them have done much to exasperate and alienate many intelligent people. Although in previous pages I may have seemed to be, and indeed up to a point was, an apologist for obscurity, confusion, and ambiguity of several sorts, my overall objective has been clarity. To this end each chapter has been cast in the form of an argument, with the arguments proceeding as logically, linearly, and sequentially as I could contrive.

If these arguments, however, suggest that they are reflections of the way by which I actually arrived at certain conclusions about Canadian history they are misleading. For I did not simply read McLuhan and then seek to apply his ideas to an interpretation of history. I had reached many of my conclusions –

about the use of the terms 'responsible government' and 'family compact,' for example – long before I read McLuhan. My conclusions, however, seemed to coincide with much of what he had to say about a medium being the message when I thought about it later.

But sometimes I attempted to adapt methods and procedures suggested by McLuhan to my own particular objectives. From time to time I have tried to demonstrate a theory, or a method, by application as I proceeded. Moreover, while I have written linearly and sequentially *within* particular chapters, the chapters themselves are not *linearly connected* to each other. Rather I have tried to *relate* them to each other as figures relate to grounds. I tried to write in such a way that early chapters in part become contexts for the chapters that succeed them. Thus they are layered rather than linearly connected. In places, however, where I thought it unlikely that readers would be able easily to recall relevant material from early chapters, I have been deliberately repetitive. I do not know whether I have succeeded in all this or not. But, if I have not, I hope I have not detracted from clarity of presentation in individual chapters.

II

This book has been a good many years in the making. It had one beginning in 1970 when I was attempting to convert my doctoral dissertation, 'Studies in Elections and Public Opinion in Upper Canada' (University of Toronto 1969) into a political history of the colony. The thesis was 538 pages in length; and I was trying to reduce it in size. But since everywhere I turned I seemed to be engaged in substantial historical revision, I was expanding the manuscript much more than I was contracting it; and this very soon got out of hand. I then decided that I should try to cut through to fundamental, if specious, underlying structures of historical interpretation. And it seemed to me that this might best be accomplished briefly in a few short articles rather than in a very large book. Certain chapters of this present book are partial products of this research. But here too I have endeavoured to be brief. Indeed, after clarity, brevity has been my overriding objective. Brevity, I hope, has made for clarity.

This book had another beginning some time in the late 1960s when I first began to teach at the University of Toronto. Professor Natalie Davis was then organizing a first-year course in which students, after being introduced to the study of history during a first term by way of lectures, were to be turned over in the second term to individual instructors who would conduct small-group seminars on topics illustrative of the historian's craft. When she invited me to join I agreed but suggested that my contribution be something other than Canadian history, with much of which I was then bored, and of which I thought I was teaching quite enough. She replied: 'Oh but Graeme, you could teach Innis.'

This proposal seemed to be perfectly crazed. In the recent past I had barely managed to drive myself through *The Fur Trade in Canada* and *The Cod Fisheries*. A reading of either of those turgid, if important, texts it seemed to me would be well calculated to alienate permanently the already pretty well alienated students of the 1960s; and a re-reading of those texts at that time would certainly have alienated me. I was then almost completely unfamiliar with the late work of Innis but, from what I had heard of it, it promised even greater disaster. Natalie Davis's suggestion, however, turned my mind to McLuhan, whose name was associated with the work of Innis and who seemed to be enjoying a huge success with undergraduates all over the world.

At that time I knew very little of the man. I possessed a copy of *Understanding Media*, which I had once begun to read but had tossed aside as nonsense. I began to read it again; and on page 25 I was hooked. 'A fairly complete handbook for studying the extensions of man,' McLuhan had written, 'could be made up from selections from Shakespeare. Some might quibble about whether or not he was referring to TV in these familiar lines from *Romeo and Juliet*:

> *But soft! what light through yonder window breaks?*
> *It speaks, and yet says nothing.'*

When I related this comment to some remarks I had heard years before in an undergraduate lecture given by Donald Creighton, I made my first breakthrough.

When delivering magisterial public lectures to his academic peers on clichéd subjects like responsible government. Creighton could be immensely entertaining and interesting; but when he lectured to undergraduates on the same clichéd subjects he could be as dull as the next fellow. This was not because he was not a conscientious teacher – he was exceedingly conscientious – but because he apparently felt obliged to present standard material in a standard way that he himself found to be less than fascinating. One day while lecturing on some such time-worn topic he stood back from his lectern and with some enthusiasm began to explain something that interested him, namely the importance of the work of Harold Innis. Before Innis, he said, scholars had studied the fur trade, the timber trade, and trade in wheat and flour. But they had treated all these commodities separately. Innis had put them all together in one unified theory that related staple commodities to a communications system. Reading McLuhan a number of years later I could see that he was doing exactly the same thing with respect both to content and to a medium of communication. He, of course, was dealing not with material content but with a content of ideas, and not with a river as a medium of communication but with a metaphor. He had made Juliet's window yield to a television screen, however, even as beaver pelts had once given way to squared timber in the commerce of the St Lawrence.

In the 1960s and early 1970s undergraduates were considerably more present-minded than they are today. They demanded 'relevance'; and what was relevant to them was mostly what had transpired in the twentieth century, particularly in the United States or Canada. In my tutorial groups I hoped to persuade them otherwise. I called the course 'Man in Society,' a then fashionable piece of jargon that could be used to include almost any conceivable historical activity. It was intended, however, to apply specifically to readings related to alienation, or lack thereof, past and present, and to the relation of the individual to society at large. Fifty per cent of these readings would be selected from the remote past; the other half would be made up of books written in the twentieth century. I intended to demonstrate the importance of relating all these readings not to one's own subjective immediate present but to proper historical contexts. I also wanted students to find the material interesting; and therefore I had not intended to include any Canadian books since they seemed to me to be considerably less interesting than what I could find elsewhere. But I ended up making an exception for McLuhan.

The readings began with *Euthyphro, the Apology*, and *The Crito* of Plato and continued through Machiavelli's *The Prince*, Sir Thomas More's *Utopia*, Voltaire's *Candide*, and Lord Chesterfield's *Letters to His Son*. Apart from *Understanding Media*, the second set of juxtaposed readings contained Jean Paul Sartre's *Anti-Semite and Jew*, Carl Jung's *Man and His Symbols*, Carl Becker's *Heavenly City of the Eighteenth-Century Philosophers* and Aldous Huxley's *Brave New World*. Of these books, McLuhan's was not the most popular. No single book was; but students generally preferred something easily read, whether taken from the remote past or the near present. The material in McLuhan's book was not easy; but it proved to be a most effective book to teach from. Oddly enough, students could be made to enjoy the book's content even when they did not particularly care for its form.

I soon discovered that the later concerns of Innis as well as those of McLuhan touched my own interests. They were interested in media of communication. Both as a historian and as a teacher I seemed to be involved with the same thing. I had long been interested in the shaping and manipulation of public opinion in Upper Canada, to which end I had made a close study of newspapers. Innis and McLuhan were interested in how opinion was formed more widely. It seemed likely that I could learn something from them. In *The Mechanical Bride* McLuhan examined ways in which advertisers and propagandists shape contemporary opinion by means of symbols and images. And sophistries of this sort, as instanced by the rhetoricians of ancient Greece and Rome, were certainly not unknown in the past. Did not this book offer valuable tools to the historian, the historiographer, and the student of politics? Innis had been interested in the political effects of the political press. Politics in Upper Canada had most certainly been profoundly affected by the press. The newspapers of Upper Canada had been studied by many other historians; but they had been almost entirely concerned with the content of those papers. Had their form, quite apart from their content, I wondered, had no effects? And I turned my mind to what these effects might have been.

When I first began to explore political life in Upper Canada, the politics of the period were generally explained as a response to grievances occasioned by a family compact. Compared to nineteenth-century writers, historians of the twentieth century had generally tended to minimize these grievances. But minimized or not they continued to be thought of as a mainspring of political activity. Moreover, in reading Upper Canadian newspapers as sceptically as I could, I was often surprised to discover how often I was deceived by them. What had been their effects, I wondered, upon readers who had not had access to other documents? What had been their effects over a number of years upon readers who not only had no access to archives but also had access to only a single partisan journal? What had been their effect upon the gossip and rumours circulating among non-readers? Political opinion, however misguided, I concluded, was more important than political grievances, however real. It was opinion, after all, that had led the rebels of 1837 to take up arms and march against a family compact.

Prior to the publication in 1963 of Gerald Craig's *Upper Canada: The Formative Years*, the basic account of the colony's history had been Aileen Dunham's *Political Unrest in Upper Canada, 1815–1836*. First published in 1927 this book had been republished in 1963 and is still in print. In 1963 it was introduced by the historian A.L. Burt who had commented: 'There is little to criticize and much to commend in Miss Dunham's book which, after nearly forty years, is now republished.'[1]

The more I examined the history of the colony the more difficult I found it to agree with this judgment. It seemed very odd that a book dealing with political unrest in Upper Canada should end one year before that unrest culminated in armed rebellion. And I found it strange that the book began in 1815, before which time Miss Dunham apparently believed the colony had had no politics. 'The justification for choosing 1815 as a starting-point,' she wrote, 'should be apparent. Before the war [of 1812] the province had no real political history; its problems were then economic. The war ushered in a more involved period, not only by increasing the population, but by concentrating British attention more fully on Canada, and by embittering relations with the United States.'[2] This view in no way coincided with my own observations of the impassioned political conflicts endemic in the colony from its origin. It seemed to be nonsense. And Miss Dunham had a most peculiar understanding of what she termed 'real political history,' to a consideration of which I will return. We must first take note, however, of the curious way her study of unrest terminated.

'Not so evident,' she allowed, 'is the reason for closing an account of political unrest in Upper Canada with the dismissal of Sir Francis Bond Head's first parliament in the summer of 1836. Against such a date it may be urged that the story has been abruptly cut off to exclude the climax, namely, the rebellion of 1837.' It was, however, precisely for this reason, she declared, that an account of 'the so-called "rebellion" ' had been omitted. 'The rebellion was not a climax, but rather an anti-climax, accidental rather than inevitable, and out of harmony with the real sentiments of Upper Canadians. To conclude this transitional period with an account of the rebellion would be to give to the most unbalanced element among the reformers, the extreme radicals, a prominence which it has been the author's deliberate purpose to avoid.' From which it would seem to follow that the rebels were not Upper Canadians.

Miss Dunham was employing a metaphor of which, in all probability, she was completely unconscious. She was conceiving of history metaphorically as a drama containing climaxes and anti-climaxes. She was not distinguishing between historical events and written history. Moreover, despite the title of her book, it was not political unrest that fundamentally concerned her. It was rather what she perceived to be the political development of the province in relation to the empire. What did she mean by declaring that the rebellion was 'accidental rather than inevitable?' Was it not, in point of fact, an event like any other? In what way did accidental events differ from inevitable ones? How could it be out of harmony with the real sentiments of at least some Upper Canadians, namely those of the rebels? Why was she marginalizing these people? The only justification for treating the rebellion, she explained, 'would be that the rebellion precipitated Lord Durham's Report and the final triumph of the idea of responsible government ...' This she evidently regarded as the real climax of her story, indeed of 'real history.' Nonetheless she was curiously uninterested in this particular climax, being only concerned with the generation of the idea of responsible government, she declared, and not with its final application.

Concerned to treat what she termed 'real political history,' Aileen Dunham averted her Whiggish eyes from political reality. The span of years from 1791 to 1837, she contended, 'is generally considered the most unattractive period of Canadian history.'[3] An opinion was prevalent that the War of 1812 and the Rebellion of 1837 alone rendered tolerable the wearisome narrative of abortive administrations and petty personal squabbles that characterized political life. Few men had leisure and ability to devote to politics, and public life was vitiated by the personal rancour inevitable in small communities. Because 'the country,' that is to say the colonies of British North America, was divided into virtually independent administrations, its history tended to be local 'and local history presents little that is grand and much that is irksome to the student.' None of this, however, appeared to her to have anything to do with 'real political history.'

A.L. Burt was a much more learned scholar than Aileen Dunham; but he and she were of one mind with respect to the overall importance of responsible government. 'One of the most interesting and instructive chapters' in her book, Burt observed,

is entitled 'The Dawn of a New Conception.' It brings out clearly what was wrong with the system of government, and how it should have been corrected ... The little oligarchy 'enjoyed a maximum of power and a minimum of responsibility.' To correct this imbalance what became known as responsible government was offered. William Warren Baldwin was the original mind that worked out the theory of responsible government in 1828. It was a remarkable achievement, for it occurred before the great reform of [the British] Parliament [of 1832]. Miss Dunham's study abundantly establishes the claim that the elder Baldwin should be regarded as the true father of responsible government.[4]

Burt and Dunham along with many others were caught up in Canadian political mythology; they were like linearly minded dreamers dreaming a dream from which they were powerless to awaken themselves. These scholars seemed to me to present a very real and very interesting problem in 'communications.'

One of the contemporaries of Burt and Dunham, Harold Innis, had either awakened from the dream or had never entertained it. In contrast to other historians who viewed a linear development of Canada as having been motivated by a quest for 'nationhood,' his 'staples theory' advanced the idea that Canada had developed so that more advanced countries could exploit its raw materials. Viewing the demand for responsible government as merely having been actuated by local demands for political patronage, he was well aware of the informing influence of Newtonian mechanics upon concepts of historical change, and he indicated the conditioning effects that words, writing, and print have upon the minds of men. He spent the last years of his life in search of alternatives. Innis's own writing was often very confusing; but, in contrast to Dunham and Burt, his mind seemed to be remarkably clear and unconfused.

Like many readers I initially found the books of both Innis and McLuhan difficult to follow. The best approach it seemed was to make what I could of Innis's footnotes and to read the works listed in McLuhan's several lengthy bibliographies. This was interesting; indeed it was like receiving a second liberal education. But it was a large and slow undertaking, which involved delving into economic theory, art criticism, literary criticism, world literature, philosophy, anthropology, history both ancient and modern, contemporary physics, and much else that would not normally be concerns of a student of pre-Confederation Canada. But it offered access to the minds of Innis and McLuhan. And the latter's writings, like crossword puzzles, became a hobby of mine.

For a number of years I had not the slightest intention of writing anything about either Innis or McLuhan. Then, I think in 1977, I received a letter from W.H. New, the editor of *Canadian Literature*, who had somehow heard of my activities. He was planning a special issue on Canadian intellectual history and wanted me to write on the relationship of Innis and McLuhan. Perfectly aware that I was then far from adequately understanding either man, I agreed. And in order better to understand McLuhan I decided to attend the weekly seminars he offered across the University of Toronto campus in an old carriage house at St Michael's College.

These seminars were interesting, stimulating, and, from my point of view, productive; but I remained unconvinced of my competence to deal with McLuhan's peculiar patterns of thought. I was sure, for example, that I did not fully understand the importance he assigned to figure/ground relationships. One day I approached him and inquired about an oar that was fastened to a wall of his seminar room. 'That oar,' I suggested, 'is figure and the wall is ground.' McLuhan agreed that such was the case. 'Well, so what?' I said. 'Well,' he replied, 'if the oar were still mounted on a boat that would be a very different ground.'

I could make little of this; indeed I was baffled. I did not say 'So what?' again; but I should have. Today I think I know what he meant. The oar came from the shell in which he had rowed when he was a student at Cambridge. Attached to the shell, in England, it was just an oar, part of a boat. But mounted on the wall of McLuhan's centre in Toronto it was a symbol, symbolic of an experience elsewhere.

Why, one might ask, did he not simply say so? To which there are two possible answers. On the one hand, he may have been using a first-rate teaching device. He had set two situations in apposition without logical connection and had left me to puzzle out their relationship. On the other hand, his own mind may simply have moved in this fashion quite naturally. And I think that this latter possibility was probably the case. McLuhan often seemed genuinely puzzled when other people's minds did not move like his own.

Since then I have reflected further on McLuhan's oar. An oar is clearly related to 'transportation,' a field of 'communications' pioneered by the early Innis. Fixed in its oarlock in England, McLuhan's trophy had been a means of transportation; but it was also then a mere material object. It had itself been transported from that ground and fastened to a new ground, the wall of the nineteenth-century carriage house that housed McLuhan's Centre for the Study of Technology and Culture. As a carriage house, it too could be associated with transportation and communications. Thus the oar could be viewed as a metaphor, mediating information of a non-material nature from an English context to a Canadian context.

Today I have no idea whether McLuhan actually thought about his oar like this or not. It does not really matter. The important thing is that I began to think in this fashion, not then but later.

Meanwhile, apart from my trouble understanding McLuhan, it soon became clear that he and Innis taken together were much too large a topic for a single essay. Therefore I dealt with Innis alone, although I made a few passing references to McLuhan, to whom I gave the final draft for comment. He found nothing in it to criticize negatively, praised it highly, and invited me to give a seminar on Innis, which I did. The article 'Harold Innis and the Writing of History,' which appeared in the Winter 1979 issue of *Canadian Literature*, is substantially the same as the first chapter in this present book.

Marshall McLuhan died in 1980. Soon after this some of his colleagues in the Department of English whom I did not then know began to plan a commemorative two-volume book of essays written by scholars specialized in the several fields in which he had taken an interest. They wanted to demonstrate his importance in each of these fields. Having read my essay on Innis in *Canadian Literature*, they invited me to make a historical contribution. This I did, and it was accepted for publication; but as time passed it became evident that the book would not soon, if ever, be published. I therefore had to decide whether to place my work in a learned journal, as David Staines, one of the editors of the intended book, very kindly encouraged me to do, or to publish it in some other form. The time seemed to have come to write a book; indeed for some time I had already been at work on a book.

Several scholars had studied Innis and McLuhan in relation to each other, but I appeared to be the only person to have considered both of them in relation to the history of Canada. I had been thinking about their work in this context for several years, and ideas that interested me were beginning to come together in new even more interesting ways. After nearly half a century it seemed time to reunite the late work with the early work of Harold Innis, and with it to relate other material to Canadian history by way of dealing with the curious ideas of Marshall McLuhan. It seemed that I was now in a position to do a good many things in the compass of a relatively small book.

III

McLuhan's approach to problems of communication was much influenced by literary criticism; and he drew special attention to Q.D. Leavis, whose *Fiction and the Reading Public* (London 1965), he claimed, had been sadly neglected. Mrs Leavis pioneered a field of criticism that examined the ways in which books and their intended readers interact upon each other. McLuhan made good use of this approach in *The Mechanical Bride*. And this was the sort of thing he appears to have had in mind when, in assailing the criticism of Northrop Frye, he contended that: 'For the literary archetypalist there is always a problem of whether *Oedipus Rex* or *Tom Jones* would have the same effect on an audience in the South Sea Islands as in Toronto.' It is also the sort of thing he himself appears either to have forgotten about, to have deliberately ignored, or to have sadly miscalculated with respect to his own intended readers when he fashioned *From Cliché to Archetype*, a book that seems not to have had very many positive effects on its relatively few readers.

I have had these considerations much in mind in writing this present book. The historiographical arguments in it are of course primarily addressed to the professional historians of Canada. But I would also like to reach a wider public, a public with an interest in Innis, McLuhan, and 'the field of communications' but possibly with little knowledge of Canadian history. I have therefore tried to indicate a historical relationship and, if possible, the 'relevance' of the history of Canada to that field of interest.

What may seem relevant to one historian may also appear to be completely irrelevant to others. Harold Innis was apparently of the opinion that a study of the river Nile and of the Tigris and Euphrates rivers in ancient Egypt and Mesopotamia could be related to a more recent commercial empire of the St Lawrence, a view that was not shared by his friend and colleague Donald Creighton. To show the relevance of Canadian history to communications theory, one must observe that written Canadian history is not alone among histories to have been shaped by peculiar patterns of thought. I have here been chiefly concerned with the history of Upper Canada, the chief weakness of which is also its great strength. The political history of Upper Canada is a simpler history than many others – eighteenth- and nine-teenth-century British and American political histories come to mind – in the sense that it has not been worked over, revised, and reinterpreted by an immense, possibly unmanageably large number of scholars. Both its written history and its historiography have been structured by models derived from English Whig history before it received the attention of Sir Lewis Namier and other revisionists. Politicians and journalists thought in Whig terms when they wrote about court parties and country parties. Within its written history, large and significant Whig patterns can be easily discerned. This is much more difficult in histories that have received greater attention from historians. Apart from these paradigms, the thought of Harold Innis, considered in relation to the history and historiography of Canada, may afford useful ideas for application elsewhere. This, to be sure, seems to be what he himself had in mind when moving from his early work in the history of Canada to his subsequent work elsewhere. His starting point, however, as he himself asserted, was the waterways of North America.

On many points both Harold Innis and Marshall McLuhan were undoubtedly mistaken; and these points have not much concerned me here. What have interested me are ideas that have too easily been dismissed as being either unfounded or irrelevant to the study of Canadian history. Chief among these has been McLuhan's understanding of figure/ground relations, which, in my opinion, should be of special interest to historians and to students of the culture of Canada of which the historians examined in this book have mostly been products. For they themselves may be clearly perceived as figures on that common ground.

Both Innis and McLuhan believed that the world was and continues to be shaped by communications systems; and if they were right that is of crucial importance in the world today. Still embedded in the consciousness of nationalists throughout the world is the idea and ideal of 'the autonomous nation state,' a concept with which they symbolically and passionately identify. This point of view stands in direct and dangerous dialectical opposition to some of McLuhan's least controversial ideas in much the way that responsible government once stood in opposition to family compact. McLuhan's metaphor of the global village, which refers to the *interdependent* modern world, has come to be generally accepted, indeed it has become a virtual cliché. The emergence of new economic and political patterns in the western European community, the 1988 free trade agreement between Canada and the United States, and, most striking of all, the structural effects of *perestroika* in eastern Europe, it can be argued, are all related to communications. The causes and effects of changes such as these are world-wide and not merely national or continental in extent.

If modern forms of communications structure and restructure the world as Innis and McLuhan thought, they also restructure the way in which people perceive the world. And, as illustrated by the historiography of Upper Canada, this latter process generally lags far behind the former. Moreover, if the interdependent modern world is antithetical to the nineteenth-century concept of the autonomous nation state, even as the Laurentian thesis stands opposed to that of the frontier, this makes for a dangerous state of affairs worthy of close study. It also makes for an interesting state of affairs, for it makes for a dialectically related interplay of ideas in conflict.

Life in the global village, then, is very different from that in the town of Mariposa, a fact that may greatly appeal to Canadian imperialists who still decline to be provincial.

NOTES

ABBREVIATIONS

AO   Archives of Ontario
MTPL Metropolitan Toronto Public Library
NA   National Archives of Canada
UTA   University of Toronto Archives

1 Harold Innis and the Interpretation of History

1 Ramsay Cook, 'La Survivance English-Canadian Style,' *The Maple Leaf Forever* (Toronto 1971), 144
2 H.A. Innis, 'The Bias of Communication,' *The Bias of Communication* (Toronto 1951) 33
3 H.A. Innis, 'The Problem of Space,' *The Bias of Communication*, 92; F.M. Cornford, 'The Invention of Space,' *Essays in Honour of Gilbert Murray* (London 1936)
4 Donald G. Creighton, 'The Decline and Fall of the Empire of the St. Lawrence,' *Towards the Discovery of Canada* (Toronto 1972), 160
5 H.A. Innis, *Empire and Communications*, rev. ed. (Toronto 1972), 5
6 Ibid., 6
7 Donald G. Creighton, *Harold Adams Innis: Portrait of a Scholar* (Toronto 1957), 112
8 J.M.S. Careless, 'Frontierism, Metropolitanism and Canadian History,' *Canadian Historical Review* 25 (1954), 14
9 V. Gordon Childe, *Canadian Journal of Economics and Political Science* 17 (1951), 98
10 Arthur Maheux, *Canadian Historical Review* 31 (1950)
11 Cook, 'La Survivance English-Canadian Style,' 154
12 Ibid., 144
13 Leslie A. Pal, 'Scholarship and the Later Innis,' *Journal of Canadian Studies* 12 (Winter 1977), 42

14 Carl Berger, *The Writing of Canadian History: Aspects of English-Canadian Historical Writing, 1900–1970* (Toronto 1976), 188
15 Innis, *Empire and Communications*, 12
16 Marshall McLuhan, 'The Later Innis,' *Queen's Quarterly* 60 (1953), 385
17 Stephen Leacock, *Baldwin, Lafontaine, Hincks: Responsible Government* (Toronto 1907), ix
18 W.M. Kilbourn, 'The Writing of Canadian History,' in C.F. Klinck, ed., *Literary History of Canada* (Toronto 1965), 499
19 Donald G. Creighton, *The Commercial Empire of the St. Lawrence* (Toronto 1937); Donald G. Creighton, *Dominion of the North* (Toronto 1944)
20 Creighton, *Dominion of the North*, 346
21 Ibid., 223–4; Donald G. Creighton, 'The Victorians and the Empire,' *Towards the Discovery of Canada*
22 Creighton, *Dominion of the North*, 378–80, 466–7
23 W.M. Kilbourn, 'The Writing of Canadian History,' 500
24 H.A. Innis, 'Great Britain, the United States and Canada,' *Changing Concepts of Time* (Toronto 1952), 115–16
25 W.T. Easterbrook, 'Innis and Economics,' *Canadian Journal of Economics and Political Science* 19 (1953), 291
26 H.A. Innis, 'Roman Law and the British Empire,' *Changing Concepts of Time*, 49
27 Innis, 'Great Britain, the United States and Canada,' 120
28 H.A. Innis, 'Political Economy in the Modern State,' *Political Economy in the Modern State* (Toronto 1946), 132–3
29 H.A. Innis, 'Industrialism and Cultural Values,' *The Bias of Communication*, 139–40
30 H.A. Innis, 'A Plea for Time,' *The Bias of Communication*, 79–80
31 H.A. Innis, 'A Critical Review,' *The Bias of Communication*, 190
32 Berger, *The Writing of Canadian History*, 190
33 H.A. Innis, 'Minerva's Owl,' *The Bias of Communication*, 11

2 McLuhan and Others on Innis

1 Donald G. Creighton, 'Towards the Discovery of Canada,' *Towards the Discovery of Canada* (Toronto 1972), 61

2 Donald G. Creighton *Harold Adams Innis: Portrait of a Scholar* (Toronto 1957), 101–2

3 W.J. Eccles, 'Edward Robert Adair,' *Canadian Historical Review* 46 (1965)

4 E.R. Adair, review article, *Canadian Historical Review* 33 (1952), 393–4

5 Marshall McLuhan, review of *Changing Concepts of Time*, in *Northern Review of Writing and the Arts in Canada* (Aug.–Sept. 1953), 44–6

6 Marshall McLuhan, 'The Later Innis,' *Queen's Quarterly* 60 (1953), 389

7 Marshall McLuhan, introduction to H.A. Innis, *The Bias of Communication* (Toronto 1964), vii

8 UTA, W.T. Easterbrook Papers, W.T. Easterbrook to Harold Innis, 30 May 1952

9 Ibid., Harold Innis to W.T. Easterbrook, 7 June 1952

10 McLuhan, introduction to *The Bias of Communication*, viii

11 Ibid., ix, 10

12 Creighton, *Innis*, 102

13 Easterbrook Papers, Harold Innis to Frank Knight, 11 May 1952

14 William Christian, ed., *The Idea File of Harold Adams Innis* (Toronto 1980), item 87, 39

15 Quoted by Christian, in ibid., xvii

16 H.A. Innis, *Empire and Communications*, rev. ed. (Toronto 1972), 5

17 Ibid., 5–6

18 Marshall McLuhan, *The Mechanical Bride: Folklore of Industrial Man* (New York 1951), vi

19 Ibid., 3

20 Ibid.

21 McLuhan, introduction to *The Bias of Communication*, ix

22 NA, H.M. McLuhan papers, Marshall McLuhan to Father [Lawrence] Shook, 20 June 1972. Used by permission of Corinne McLuhan

23 Marshall McLuhan, *The Gutenberg Galaxy: The Making of Typographic Man* (Toronto 1962), 50

24 Ibid.

25 McLuhan, introduction to *The Bias of Communication*, x

26 Marshall McLuhan, *Understanding Media: The Extensions of Man*
2nd ed. (New York and Scarborough 1964), 23–4

27 McLuhan, foreword to *Empire and Communications*, vii–viii

28 Ibid., viii–ix

29 Ibid., ix

30 Carl Berger, *The Writing of Canadian History: Aspects of
English-Canadian Historical Writing, 1900–1970* (Toronto
1976), 194–5

31 McLuhan, introduction to *The Bias of Communication*, vii–viii

32 W.J. Eccles, 'A Belated Review of Harold Adams Innis, The Fur
Trade in Canada,' *Canadian Historical Review* 60 (1979)

33 Ibid., 420

34 Ibid., 441

35 H.A. Innis, *The Fur Trade in Canada: An Introduction to Canadian
Economic History* (New Haven 1930; rev. ed., Toronto 1956),
383

36 J.B. Brebner, 'Harold Adams Innis as Historian,' Canadian Historical Association, *Report* (1953), 18

37 Ibid., 17

38 Ibid.

39 Berger, *The Writing of Canadian History*, 190

40 Brebner, 'Harold Adams Innis as Historian,' 20

41 Ibid., 14

42 Ibid., 14–15

43 Ibid., 15

44 Quoted by Roy Allen Billington, in *The American Frontier*, 2nd ed.
(Washington 1965), 7

45 Frederick Jackson Turner, 'The Significance of the Frontier in
American History,' *The Frontier in American History* (New York
1920), 23

46 Ibid., 4

47 W.J. Eccles, *The Canadian Frontier, 1534–1760* (New York 1969), 1

48 Ibid., 3

49 Ibid., 5

50 Roy Allen Billington, foreword to Eccles's *The Canadian Frontier*,
vii

51 Eccles, *The Canadian Frontier*, ix

52 Marshall McLuhan with Wilfred Watson, *From Cliché to Archetype* (New York 1970), 118

53 J.M.S. Careless, 'Frontierism, Metropolitanism and Canadian History,' *Canadian Historical Review* 25 (1954), 7

54 Ibid., 1

55 Donald Swainson, introduction to J.C. Dent, *The Last Forty Years: The Union of 1841 to Confederation*, Carleton Library edition (Toronto 1972), xviii

56 Donald G. Creighton, 'Macdonald and Canadian Historians,' *Towards the Discovery of Canada*, 200

57 Ibid., 198–9

3 Concepts, Models, and Metaphors

1 William Christian, ed., *The Idea File of Harold Adams Innis* (Toronto 1980), item 15/17, 125

2 Eric A. Havelock, *Harold A. Innis: A Memoir* (Toronto 1982), 39–43

3 UTA, H.A. Innis Papers, [Harold Innis] to Frank H. Knight, 21 May 1951

4 Havelock, *Harold A. Innis*, 39–40

5 Ibid., 41

6 H.A. Innis, *Changing Concepts of Time* (Toronto 1952), v

7 Eric A. Havelock, *The Crucifixion of Intellectual Man* (Boston 1951), 14

8 Ibid., 16

9 Ibid., 17

10 Ibid., 6

11 Dudley Shapere, 'Newtonian Mechanics and Mechanical Explanation,' *The Encyclopedia of Philosophy*, ed. Paul Edwards, vol. 5 (New York and London 1967), 495

12 G.J. Whitrow, 'Einstein, Albert,' *The Encyclopedia of Philosophy*, vol. 2, 470

13 H.A. Innis, 'A Critical Review,' *The Bias of Communication* (Toronto 1951) 190

14 H.A. Innis, 'The Problem of Space,' *The Bias of Communication*, 92

15 Francis Cornford, 'The Invention of Space,' *Essays in Honour of Gilbert Murray* (London 1936), 215–16

16 Ibid., 234–5
17 Ernst Cassirer, *The Problem of Knowledge: Philosophy, Science and History since Hegel* (New Haven 1950), 23
18 Ibid., 24
19 Ibid., 21
20 Ibid., 37
21 Ibid., 97–8
22 H.A. Innis, review article, *Canadian Geographical Journal* 27 (Dec. 1943), xv
23 UTA, H.A. Innis Papers, H.A. Innis to John Gray, 23 July 1952
24 Ibid., Harold Innis to Don[ald] and Luella Creighton, 11 May 1952
25 Donald G. Creighton, 'The Commercial Class in Canadian Politics, 1792–1840,' *Papers and Proceedings of the Canadian Political Science Association* 5 (May 1933), 43–58, quotation on 43
26 Ibid., 86
27 Donald G. Creighton, 'The Struggle for Financial Control in Lower Canada, 1818–1831,' *Canadian Historical Review* 12 (June 1931), 144
28 J.B. Bury, *The Idea of Progress: An Inquiry into Its Origin and Growth* (London 1928), 4
29 Herbert Butterfield, *The Whig Interpretation of History*, Norton Library edition (London 1965), v
30 Donald G. Creighton, 'History and Literature,' *Towards the Discovery of Canada* (Toronto 1972), 26
31 Donald G. Creighton, 'Macdonald and Canadian Historians,' *Towards the Discovery of Canada*, 201
32 NA, D.G. Creighton Papers, undated manuscript, MG 31 D 77, vol. 63
33 C.P. Lucas, ed., *Lord Durham's Report on the Affairs of British North America*, vol. 2 (Oxford 1915), 31
34 Northrop Frye, *Anatomy of Criticism: Four Essays* (New York 1970), 102
35 Creighton, 'History and Literature,' 18
36 Creighton, 'The Commercial Class in Canadian Politics,' 100
37 H.A. Innis, 'Great Britain, the United States and Canada,' *Changing Concepts of Time*, 120

38 Donald G. Creighton, 'The Use and Abuse of History,' *Towards the Discovery of Canada*, 69–70

39 Donald G. Creighton, *Dominion of the North* (Toronto 1944), 315

40 Ibid., 316

41 Donald G. Creighton, 'Macdonald, Confederation and the West,' *Towards the Discovery of Canada*, 236

42 Creighton, 'History and Literature,' 23

43 T.S. Eliot, *The Complete Plays and Poems* (New York 1952), 52, n 218

44 William James, *The Principles of Psychology*, vol. 1 (New York 1890), 239

45 Denis Donoghue, 'Feelings of And and If, Of and But,' *New York Times Book Review* 25 Jan 1987, 10

46 H.A. Innis, 'Minerva's Owl,' *The Bias of Communication*, 3

47 Ibid., 30

48 Claude E. Shannon and Warren Weaver, *The Mathematical Theory of Communication* (Urbana, Ill. 1964), 7

49 Ibid., 25

50 NA, H.M. McLuhan Papers, H.M. McLuhan to Jerry Agel, 26 Mar. 1976. Used by permission of Corinne McLuhan

4 Archetypal Criticism

1 John Fowles, review article, *Saturday Review* 21 Nov. 1970, 33–4

2 Marshall McLuhan with Wilfred Watson, *From Cliché to Archetype* (New York 1970), 121

3 Marshall McLuhan, *Understanding Media: The Extensions of Man*, 2nd ed. (New York and Scarborough 1964), 25

4 Ibid., xi

5 Marshall McLuhan, 'Pound's Critical Prose,' *The Interior Landscape: The Literary Criticism of Marshall McLuhan*, ed. Eugene McNamara (New York 1969), 80

6 Ibid., 79–80

7 Hugh Kenner, *New York Times Book Review* 13 Dec. 1970, 7

8 C.G. Jung, *The Archetypes and the Collective Unconscious*, *The Collected Works of C.G. Jung*, ed. Sir Herbert Read, Michael Ford-

ham, Gerhard Adler, vol. 9, trans. R.F.C Hull, part 1 (London 1959), 4

9 *Webster's Third New International Dictionary of the English Language Unabridged* (New York 1961)

10 André Gide, as quoted in *Le Grand Robert de la langue française* vol. 1, 2nd ed. (Paris 1985), 517

11 Andrew Samuels, Bani Shorter, and Fred Plaut, *A Critical Dictionary of Jungian Analysis* (London 1986), 26–8

12 Northrop Frye, *The Critical Path: An Essay on the Social Context of Literary Criticism* (Bloomington and London 1971), 16

13 Joseph Campbell, *The Hero with a Thousand Faces* (Princeton 1949), 18, n18

14 Mircea Eliade, *Cosmos and History: The Myth of the Eternal Return* (New York 1959), viii–ix

15 Beverly Moon, 'Archetypes,' in Mircea Eliade, ed. *Encyclopedia of Religion*, vol. 1 (New York 1984), 380

16 Ibid., 380–1

17 Lauriat Lane, Jr, 'The Literary Archetype: Some Reconsiderations,' *Journal of Aesthetics and Art Criticism* 13 (1954–5), 226–32

18 Northrop Frye, *Anatomy of Criticism: Four Essays* (New York 1970), 365

19 Northrop Frye, Sheridan Baker, and George Perkins, *The Harper Handbook to Literature* (New York 1985)

20 NA, H.M. McLuhan Papers, H.M. McLuhan to Henry Overduin, 1 Nov. 1971. Used by permission of Corinne McLuhan

21 H.W. Fowler, *A Dictionary of Modern English Usage* (Oxford 1937), with corrections, 348–9

22 NA, H.M. McLuhan Papers, Wilfred [Watson] to H.M. McLuhan, 29 June 1964

23 Ibid., H.M. McLuhan to Wilfred [Watson], 16 July 1964. Used by permission of Corinne McLuhan

24 Ibid., H.M. McLuhan to Sheila [Watson], 28 Dec. 1965. Used by permission of Corinne McLuhan

25 McLuhan, *From Cliché to Archetype*, 18

26 NA, H.M. McLuhan Papers, H.M. McLuhan to Wilfred [Watson], 30 June 1965. Used by permission of Corinne McLuhan

27 McLuhan, *From Cliché to Archetype*, 117

28 T.S. Eliot, *Selected Essays, 1917–1932*, 3rd ed. (New York 1950), 155

29 McLuhan, *From Cliché to Archetype*, 118

30 Frye, *Anatomy of Criticism*, 111–12

31 McLuhan, *From Cliché to Archetype*, 118

32 Frye, *Anatomy of Criticism*, 13

33 Ibid., 96

34 Ibid., 246–7

35 McLuhan, *From Cliché to Archetype*, 86

36 Ibid., 87

37 Frye, *Anatomy of Criticism*, 367

38 Ibid., 99

39 McLuhan, *From Cliché to Archetype*, 36

40 C.G. Jung, *Psychological Types, Collected Works*, vol. 6, 474

41 McLuhan, *From Cliché to Archetype*, 19–20

42 NA, H.M. McLuhan Papers, H.M. McLuhan to Walter J. Ong, sj, and Clement J. McNaspy, sj, 23 Dec. 1944. See also Matie Molinaro, Corinne McLuhan, and William Toye, eds., *Letters of Marshall McLuhan* (Toronto, Oxford, New York 1987), 166.

43 McLuhan, *From Cliché to Archetype*, 126–7

5 Formal Causality Applied

1 Richard Taylor, 'Causation,' *The Encyclopedia of Philosophy*, vol. 2 (New York 1967), 56

2 NA, H.M. McLuhan Papers, [H.M. McLuhan] to Peter Drucker, 15 Dec. 1959. See also Matie Molinaro, Corinne McLuhan, and William Toye, *Letters of Marshall McLuhan* (Toronto, Oxford, New York 1987), 259–60

3 Marshall McLuhan, introduction to H.A. Innis, *The Bias of Communication* (Toronto 1951), x

4 W.S. Wallace, *The Family Compact* (Toronto 1915), 28–9

5 A. Ewart and J. Jarvis, 'The Personnel of the Family Compact,' *Canadian Historical Review* 7 (1926), 209–19

6 Aileen Dunham, *Political Unrest in Upper Canada, 1815–1836* (London 1927; Toronto 1963), 44

7 Donald G. Creighton, *The Commercial Empire of the St. Lawrence*,

1760–1850 (Toronto 1937, republished as *The Empire of the St. Lawrence*, Toronto 1956), 265

8 Hugh Aitken, 'The Family Compact and the Welland Canal Company,' *Canadian Journal of Economics and Political Science* 18 (1952), 63–76

9 R.E. Saunders, 'What Was the Family Compact?' *Ontario History* 49 (1957), 165–78

10 S.F. Wise, 'The Rise of Christopher Hagerman,' *Historic Kingston* (1966); 'Tory Factionalism: Kingston Elections and Upper Canadian Politics, 1820–1836,' *Ontario History* 57 (1965); 205–28; 'Upper Canada and the Conservative Tradition,' *Profiles of a Province* (Toronto 1967)

11 Gerald M. Craig, *Upper Canada: The Formative Years* (Toronto 1963), 107

12 S.F. Wise, 'The Origins of Anti-Americanism in Canada,' reprinted as 'The Family Compact: A Negative Oligarchy,' in D.W. Earl, ed., *The Family Compact: Aristocracy or Oligarchy?* (Toronto 1967), 143

13 S.F. Wise, 'Upper Canada and the Conservative Tradition,' 21

14 Kenneth Windsor, 'Historical Writing in Canada to 1820,' in C.F. Klinck, ed., *Literary History of Canada* (Toronto 1965), 231

15 Dunham, *Political Unrest in Upper Canada*, 156

16 W.P.M. Kennedy, ed., *Statutes, Treaties and Documents of the Canadian Constitution* (Oxford 1930), Craig to Castlereagh, 5 Aug. 1808, 224

17 Fernand Ouellet, 'La Naissance des partis politiques dans le Bas-Canada,' *Eléments d'histoire sociale du Bas-Canada* (Montréal 1972), 206

18 Ibid., 222

19 Chester Martin, *Empire and Commonwealth* (Oxford 1925)

20 Quoted in Charles Petrie, *King Charles III of Spain* (London 1971), 116

21 Barnabas Bidwell, *The Honorable Mr. Sedgewick's Political Last Will and Testament* (n.p. 1800), 7–8

22 Barnabas Bidwell, *An Oration, Delivered at the Celebration of American Independence* (Stockbridge, Mass. 1795), 18

23 S.F. Wise, 'Kingston Elections and Upper Canadian Politics,' 214, n33

24 MTPL, W.W. Baldwin Papers, M.S. Bidwell to W.W. Baldwin, 8 Sept. 1828
25 *Weekly Register* 9 Oct. 1823
26 *Upper Canada Herald* 17 May 1825
27 Ibid., 7 June 1825, letter of 'A Plough Jogger'
28 W.L. Mackenzie, 'Upper Canada – King, Lords and Commons,' *Sketches of Upper Canada and the United States* (London 1833)
29 Ibid., 409
30 C.P. Lucas, ed., *Lord Durham's Report on the Affairs of British North America*, vol. 2 (Oxford 1912), 148
31 AO, Mackenzie-Lindsey Collection, item 1009, newspaper clipping
32 Windsor, 'Historical Writing in Canada to 1820,' 216; J.M. McMullen, *The History of Canada* (Brockville, Ont. 1855)
33 McMullen, *The History of Canada*, 234
34 Ibid., 235
35 Ibid., 235–6
36 Ibid., 499
37 Louis Turcotte, *Le Canada sous l'union, 1841–1867* (Quebec 1871), 39
38 Ibid., 78
39 Ibid., 80
40 Ibid., 86
41 Egerton Ryerson, *Sir Charles Metcalfe Defended against the Attacks of His Late Councillors* (Toronto 1844)
42 *Examiner* 3 July 1838: see the quotation appended to the masthead of this and other issues.
43 Francis Hincks, *Reminiscence of His Public Life* (Montreal 1844), 47
44 Ibid.
45 Mircea Eliade, *Myth and Reality* (New York 1963), 1
46 G.H. Patterson, 'Studies in Elections and Public Opinion in Upper Canada' (PHD, diss., University of Toronto 1969)

6 Comparisons

1 H.A. Innis, 'Minerva's Owl,' *The Bias of Communication* (Toronto 1951), 11

2 Thomas S. Kuhn, *The Structure of Scientific Revolutions* (Chicago 1962)

3 Ibid., x

4 H.A Innis, 'A Critical Review,' *The Bias of Communication*, 190

5 Robert Coover, 'He Thinks the Way We Dream,' *New York Times Book Review* 20 Nov. 1988, 15

6 T.S. Eliot, 'Burnt Norton,' *The Complete Poems and Plays* (New York 1952), 117

7 H.A. Innis, 'The Problem of Space,' *The Bias of Communication*, 92

8 NA, H.M. McLuhan Papers, undated note, vol. 116, file 1. Used by permission of Corinne McLuhan

9 Gerald M. Craig, *Upper Canada: The Formative Years* (Toronto 1963), 107

10 Quoted in David Mills, *The Idea of Loyalty in Upper Canada 1784–1850* (Kingston and Montreal 1988), 78

11 Quoted in Donald C. MacDonald, 'Honourable Richard Cartwright, 1759–1815,' in *Three History Theses*, Ontario Department of Public Records and Archives (Toronto 1961), 66

12 Norfolk Historical Society, Thomas Welch papers, Thomas Welch to William Halton, 11 Nov. 1807

13 James H. Coyne, ed., 'The Talbot Papers,' *Transactions of the Royal Society of Canada*, sec. 2 (1909), Col. Talbot to Hon. Peter Robinson, 15 Apr. 1830, 110

14 *Liberal* 15 Nov. 1832

15 NA, Upper Canada Sundries, Alex. Ross to J. Joseph, 22 June 1836

16 Stephen Leacock, *Sunshine Sketches of a Little Town* (Toronto 1960), xvi

17 Ibid., 124

18 Ibid., 125

19 *Globe* 4 Nov. 1851

20 Stephen Leacock, *Baldwin, Lafontaine, Hincks: Responsible Government* (Toronto 1907), ix

21 Stephen Leacock, 'Reader's Junk,' *Too Much College: Or Education Eating up Life* (New York 1939), 191–3

22 Leacock, *Sunshine Sketches*, 5–6

23 A.B. McKillop, ed., *A Critical Spirit: The Thought of William Dawson*

LeSueur (Toronto 1977), W.D. LeSueur to Stephen Leacock, 26 Oct. 1906, 272

24 Stephen Leacock, *Mackenzie, Baldwin, Lafontaine, Hincks* (London and Toronto 1926), unpaginated editor's preface

25 Stephen Leacock, *The British Empire* (New York 1940), 158–9

26 Donald G. Creighton, *Harold Adams Innis: Portrait of a Scholar* (Toronto 1957), 134–5

27 H.A. Innis, *Empire and Communications*, rev. ed. (Toronto 1972), 3

28 H.A. Innis, review article, *Canadian Geographical Journal* 27 (Dec. 1943), xv

Afterword

1 Aileen Dunham, *Political Unrest in Upper Canada, 1815–1836* (London 1927; Toronto 1963), xi

2 Ibid., 18

3 Ibid., 15

4 Ibid., xiv

INDEX